T0345320

Jane Austen

The Chawton Letters

Jane Austen

The Chawton Letters

EDITED WITH AN INTRODUCTION BY

KATHRYN SUTHERLAND

Bodleian Library
UNIVERSITY OF OXFORD

JANE AUSTEN'S
HOUSE MUSEUM

First published in 2018 by the Bodleian Library
Broad Street, Oxford OX1 3BG
in association with Jane Austen's House Museum

www.bodleianshop.co.uk

ISBN 978 1 85124 474 4

Cover design by Dot Little at the Bodleian Library
Designed and typeset by Laura Parker in DTL Elzevir
Printed and bound in Italy by L.E.G.O. SpA on 130 gsm Munken Pure paper

British Library Catalogue in Publishing Data

A CIP record of this publication is available from the British Library

CONTENTS

6
Acknowledgements

———◆———

9
Chronology

———◆———

15
Introduction

———◆———

33
Letters

———◆———

126
Further Reading

———◆———

127
Index

Acknowledgements

I am grateful to Professor Richard Jenkyns, Chairman of the Jane Austen Society, for permission to transcribe and include here Austen's letter of 26 May 1801. All other letters are freshly transcribed from the original documents now held by Jane Austen's House Museum. My thanks to Isabel Snowden, Collections Officer at the Museum, for advice and assistance.

The Museum was opened in 1949, thanks to the generosity of T. Edward Carpenter, who purchased Jane Austen's former home and oversaw its transformation into a memorial to the novelist. In the previous year, Carpenter had acquired from the rare book and manuscript dealers Maggs and Quaritch several of Austen's letters that had recently come onto the market. These particular letters had remained in family hands until the 1920s, by which time they were the property of Charles Austen's granddaughters, who sold them to the collector Frederick R. Lovering. The Lovering collection was auctioned at Sotheby's, London, on 3 May 1948. On 10 May 1948, Dorothy Darnell, founder-member, in 1940, of the Jane Austen Society, wrote to Carpenter expressing her thanks for his purchase of the letters and outlining her idea of what belongs in a writer's house museum: 'I am simply thrilled with all that you are accomplishing &

the possession of the letters is *quite* wonderful … I agree with you that we should consider mainly those things that are really connected with her personally.'[1] Carpenter's letters, bequeathed to the Museum in 1969, stand high among such 'things that are really connected with her personally'; they form the heart of the collection published here. Those wishing to read more of Austen's letters should turn to Deirdre Le Faye's authoritative edition, *Jane Austen's Letters*, 4th edition, Oxford University Press, Oxford, 2011.

Kathryn Sutherland
Trustee, Jane Austen's House Museum

NOTE
1   Jane Austen's House Museum, Archive of the Jane Austen Memorial Trust, item 221.

Chronology

1773	(9 Jan.) Cassandra Austen born at Steventon, Hampshire.
1775	(16 Dec.) JA born at Steventon.
1785–6	JA and Cassandra attend the Abbey House School, Reading.
1787–93	JA writing mini-novels, plays, humorous sketches for family entertainment and collecting them in three manuscript notebooks, grandly titled 'Volume the First', 'Volume the Second' and 'Volume the Third'.
1795	JA writes 'Elinor and Marianne' (an early draft of *Sense and Sensibility*); probably working on 'Lady Susan'.
1796	(Jan.) JA's earliest surviving letter, to Cassandra Austen; Oct., begins 'First Impressions' (finished Aug. 1797; later revised and published as *Pride and Prejudice*).
1798	JA begins writing 'Susan' (*Northanger Abbey*).
1800	Mrs Leigh Perrot, JA's aunt, tried at Taunton on a charge of theft and acquitted.

1801	(May) Austens leave Steventon and settle in Bath on Revd George Austen's retirement.
1801	❧ *Letter 1: 26–27 May 1801, JA to Cassandra Austen, from Bath to Kintbury, Berkshire*
1802	(2 Dec.) Harris Bigg-Wither, brother of JA's friends, Elizabeth, Catherine and Alethea Bigg, proposes and is accepted, only to be immediately rejected; JA revises 'Susan' (*Northanger Abbey*).
1803	JA sells 'Susan' to Crosby and Co. for £10.
1804–5	JA writing 'The Watsons' (unfinished) and continuing 'Lady Susan', both unpublished in her lifetime. (Jan. 1805) death of Revd George Austen in Bath; Martha Lloyd joins the Austen household.
1806	(Oct.) Austens take lodgings in Southampton with JA's brother Frank and his new wife.
1807	(March) Austens move into a house in Castle Square, Southampton.
	❧ *Letter 2: 26 August 1808, JA's poem-letter to Catherine Bigg*

1809	(July) Austens move to Chawton Cottage, Hampshire, owned by JA's brother Edward.
	⮞ *Letter 3: JA's poem-letter to Frank Austen, 26 July 1809, from Chawton to China*
1810	*Sense and Sensibility* accepted for publication by Thomas Egerton.
1811	(Feb.) JA planning *Mansfield Park*; (30 Oct.) *Sense and Sensibility* published; (?winter) JA begins revising 'First Impressions' as *Pride and Prejudice*.
1812	Edward Austen officially takes name of Knight; (autumn) JA sells copyright of *Pride and Prejudice* to Egerton for £110.
1813	(28 Jan.) *Pride and Prejudice* published; (?July) JA finishes *Mansfield Park*.
	⮞ *Letters 4–7: January–February 1813, JA to Cassandra Austen, four letters from Chawton to Steventon and Manydown, Hampshire;*
	⮞ *Letter 8: 20 May 1813, JA to Cassandra Austen, from London to Chawton*
1814	(21 Jan.) JA begins *Emma*; (9 May) *Mansfield Park* published by Egerton.

❧ Letter 9: 2–3 March 1814, JA to Cassandra Austen, from London to Chawton

1815   (29 March) *Emma* finished; (8 Aug.) JA begins *Persuasion*; (Oct.) in London nursing Henry Austen who is ill; (13 Nov.) visits the Prince Regent's Library at Carlton House; (Dec.) *Emma* (dedicated to Regent) published by John Murray (title page dated 1816).

1816   (Spring) JA's health begins to fail; Henry buys back manuscript of 'Susan', which JA revises (as 'Catherine'); (6 Aug.) *Persuasion* finished.

❧ Letters 10–12: 11 December 1815–1 April 1816, between JA and James Stanier Clarke, addressed from London, Brighton and Chawton

1817   (27 Jan.–18 March) JA at work on 'Sanditon'; (27 April) JA makes her will; (24 May) Cassandra takes JA for medical care to Winchester, where they lodge at 8 College Street; (18 July) JA dies in early morning; (24 July) JA buried in Winchester Cathedral; (Dec.) *Northanger Abbey* (previously titled 'Susan' and 'Catherine') and *Persuasion* published together by Murray (title page dated 1818), with Henry Austen's 'Biographical Notice of the Author', the first public identification of JA with the novels.

1817	❧ *Letter 13: 29 July 1817, Cassandra Austen to Fanny Knight, from Chawton to Godmersham, Kent*
1845	(22 March) Cassandra Austen dies and JA's manuscripts and letters are divided among the family.
1884	*Letters of Jane Austen*, edited by her great-nephew Lord Brabourne, son of Fanny Knight.
1906	*Jane Austen's Sailor Brothers*, by J.H. and E.C. Hubback, JA's great-nephew and great-great niece; first publication of her letters to Frank Austen.
1932	*Jane Austen's Letters*, ed. R.W. Chapman, Oxford University Press, Oxford.
1940	The Jane Austen Society is founded.
1948	Chawton Cottage, JA's last home, is purchased by T. Edward Carpenter.
1949	The Museum in Chawton opens under the management of the Jane Austen Memorial Trust.
2014	The Jane Austen Memorial Trust transfers to the Jane Austen's House Museum CIO.

Introduction

Her letters are the only evidence we have of Jane Austen speaking/writing in her own voice: no diaries or journals survive confiding her innermost thoughts or fears in private to the page. Unmediated by fiction, the letters draw us closer to the world in which she moved, but they yield few personal secrets. That said, in detail and tone the letters bring into sharper focus the myriad interconnections between life and fiction; such insights alone make them precious. Henry Austen, in his 'Biographical Notice of the Author' (1818), written to introduce *Northanger Abbey* and *Persuasion*, the two novels left unpublished at her early death in 1817, rooted his sister's talents as fiction maker in an aptitude for writing letters: 'The style of her familiar correspondence was in all respects the same as that of her novels.'[1] In part, he wished to defend Austen from the taint of professionalism: the charge that she laboured in unladylike fashion over the novels – something she clearly did do, as several of the letters collected here show. But this does not mean there is no truth in what he suggests: that an identifiable style and subject matter knit these chatty, familiar letters to the highly manufactured novels. It is not that she talks in the letters a great deal about the business of writing fiction – she does do so on occasion and we wish she did it more frequently – but that we hear the same range of social preoccupations across both. Austen defended the ground of her fiction in a letter reproduced here, written to James Stanier Clarke, librarian to the Prince Regent, who urged her, somewhat improbably, to write a historical romance about the royal family. She replied politely but firmly, that 'I must keep to my own style & go on in my own Way', which was to 'deal in' 'pictures of domestic Life in Country Villages' (1 April 1816). It is a description that applies with equal truth to the bulk of her letters, written between the great houses, rectories and more modest dwellings of rural southern England.

In several letters we meet immediate family and members of the wider circle amongst whom Austen regularly moved – brothers, sister, mother, sisters-in-law, uncle and aunt, friends and neighbours. We glimpse household arrangements in the cottage in Chawton, Hampshire, Austen's home from 1809: cook fussing over the brewing of the mead; Betsey, the maid, who sends oranges to Steventon, brother James's home 16 miles away; the manservant, 'my own dear Thomas', who walks Jane back at night from the neighbours'; Browning, 'quite a new broom', who steps into Thomas's duties on his

FACING Postman from William Alexander, *Picturesque representations of the dress and manners of the English*, 1814. The red wax seals on the letters are visible in the illustration.

ENGLAND — PLATE 24.

marriage; even the dogs get a mention. We enter a daily round of visiting, dining out, drinking tea, reading clubs and book exchanges, walking to the shops and sending to the post. We learn the cost of a pair of gloves, the best route by carriage from Chawton to London, and that veal cutlets and cold ham make a good 3 o'clock dinner on the road. This world shares social boundaries, activities and values not only with that of Austen's novels of life among the gentry and the propertied professional classes in the early nineteenth century, but with so much women's fiction of the last two hundred years: with the middle-class fiction of Virginia Woolf, Barbara Pym and Joanna Trollope. Domestic letter writing, too, of course, is, by tradition, a female employment, and it is no coincidence that early experiments in the novel, among them Austen's own, were written as series of letters.

A preoccupation of both letters and novel is the adequate accounting of everyday life; the challenge of both is to discover a proper sense of what signifies among the myriad events of a day. A letter dated 18–20 April 1811, sent by Austen from Sloane Street, London, gestures in its opening words to this vital link with her novels: 'My dear Cassandra,' she writes there, 'I have so many little matters to tell you of.' 'Little matters' is an apt summary of the ingredients of Austen's domestic letters *and* her domestic novels; in each case, the reader must distinguish the momentous 'little matter', the small detail that, unpacked, yields so much more than at first appears, from the merely trivial, spoken to fill the silence or written to fill the page. In a letter it means weighing the relative import of an uncle's 'broken Chilblain', a brother's safe arrival at his ship and the fact that it is yet again raining. In a novel it means teasing out the significance of Frank Churchill's rapt absorption in 'fastening in the rivet of [Mrs Bates's] spectacles' and Mr Knightley's gift of the last of his apples to tempt Jane Fairfax's small appetite (*Emma*, ch. 27).

Those who would dismiss the chattering Miss Bates, Highbury's most vocal spinster, as Emma Woodhouse too readily does, as a tedious bore, should note that Austen introduces her in words that echo those she chose to sum up her own concerns in writing to her sister Cassandra: Miss Bates, too, 'was a great talker upon little matters' (*Emma*, ch. 3). In the tumbled, associative stream that characterizes her compressed, telegraphic style of speaking, Miss Bates comes very close to Austen's way of writing in her most familiar letters; in novel as in letters there is a calculated art behind the seeming artlessness. Here is Miss Bates:

> The rivet came out, you know, this morning.—
> So very obliging!—For my mother had no use
> of her spectacles—could not put them on. And,
> by the bye, every body ought to have two pair
> of spectacles; they should indeed. Jane said so.
> I meant to take them over to John Saunders
> the first thing I did, but something or other
> hindered me all the morning; first one thing,

then another, there is no saying what, you know. At one time Patty came to say she thought the chimney wanted sweeping. Oh! Said I, Patty do not come with your bad news to me. Here is the rivet of your mistress's spectacles out. Then the baked apples came home, Mrs Wallis sent them by her boy; they are extremely civil and obliging to us, the Wallises, always—I have heard some people say that Mrs Wallis can be uncivil and give a very rude answer, but we have never known any thing but the greatest attention from them. And it cannot be for the value of our custom now, for what is our consumption of bread, you know? Only three of us—besides dear Jane at present—and she really eats nothing—makes such a shocking breakfast, you would be quite frightened if you saw it. I dare not let my mother know how little she eats—so I say one thing and then I say another, and it passes off. (*Emma*, ch. 27)

Here is Jane Austen in full flow:

We admire your Charades excessively, but as yet have guessed only the 1st. The others seem very difficult. There is so much beauty in the versification however, that the finding them

out is but a secondary pleasure.—I grant you
that <u>this is</u> a cold day, & am sorry to think
how cold you will be through the process of
your visit at Manydown. I hope you will wear
your China Crape. Poor wretch! I can see you
shivering away, with your miserable feeling
feet.—What a vile Character Mr Digweed turns
out; quite beyond anything & everything;—
instead of going to Steventon they are to have a
Dinnerparty next tuesday!—I am sorry to say
that I could not eat a Mincepie at Mr Papillon's;
I was rather head-achey that day, & c^d not
venture on anything sweet except Jelly; but <u>that</u>
was excellent.—There were no stewed pears;
but Miss Benn had some almonds & raisins.—
By the bye, she desired to be kindly remembered
to you when I wrote last, & I forgot it.—
(29 January 1813)

Perhaps it is no coincidence that, among the novels, it is
Emma that singles out the Post Office for particular praise:

'The post-office is a wonderful establishment!'
said [Jane Fairfax].—'The regularity and
dispatch of it! If one thinks of all that it has
to do, and all that it does so well, it is really
astonishing!' (ch. 34)

Austen's is a predominantly domestic and social correspondence, carried on with Cassandra Austen and extending in later years to the elder of her nieces and nephews. Its chief function was to maintain family connections and to share news, where news can be as trivial as the London fashion for wearing veils or as momentous as the celebration of a birth or a brother's promotion or, for the modern reader, rare glimpses into the early reception within the family circle of her latest novel. The voice of the letters, like their subject matter, shifts with the correspondent. Those to Cassandra are certainly Austen's most intimate and least guarded, addressing one whose sympathy, on almost any topic, could be taken for granted. For this reason, they can be difficult for the modern reader to decode: the shared jokes, views on books, family members and neighbours. The sisters draw on deep reserves of mutual understanding that leave much unstated or merely hinted at because so well understood between them. To Cassandra, Austen is humorous, self-critical and, on occasion, openly cruel in her comments on others, writing in the full certainty that this special reader will laugh and forgive the odd outrageous remark: 'Mrs Bramstone is the sort of Woman I detest' (24 January 1813); 'Kill poor Mrs Sclater if you like it, while you are at Manydown' (9 February 1813).

FACING Lady in morning dress, fashion plate published by Ackermann, May 1813.

That said, Jane's letters to Cassandra are not private epistles for her eyes only; rather, they are newsletters. Jane and Cassandra Austen were, by convention, delegated to write the open letters – a mix of news, gossip and opinion – that kept one family group in touch with another. Though the sisters wrote personally to each other, they also wrote as representatives of the households they inhabited, whether that was their shared home in Chawton or the household that one or other of them was visiting at the time: brother Henry's various homes in the fashionable parts of London or brother Edward's grand estate at Godmersham, Kent. Unmarried dependants, the two sisters fulfilled an important role in travelling and corresponding between the branches of their extended family. The arrival of a letter from one sister to the other would be a social event in itself as much as a record of events happening elsewhere: it would be read aloud, commented on and passed from hand to hand, much as are the letters that arrive from Jane Fairfax or Frank Churchill in the epistolary subplots of *Emma*. Even so, it is tempting to detect in the note-like style, the darting from topic to topic – that in extreme form distinguishes the letters to Cassandra – a discontinuity that might, on occasion, have allowed the recipient to censor what she shared, moving swiftly over portions that indeed may have been for her eyes only.

That Jane Austen's letters survive in any quantity is largely thanks to Cassandra. Their niece, Caroline Austen, described how some time in the 1840s Aunt Cassandra 'looked them over and burnt' the bulk of her correspondence from her sister: 'She left, or *gave* some as legacies to the Nieces – but of those that *I* have seen, several had portions cut out.'[2] There are, at the latest count, 160 letters extant (161 when Austen's last will is included) out of an original correspondence that can be estimated, using patterns of letter production established in the more active periods of communication, at around 3,000 letters. Ninety-four of these surviving letters are from Jane to Cassandra. Typically, the sisters sent two letters each per week when they were apart, each perhaps written over two or three days, the next often begun within hours of the latest sent, rather than in response to the direct promptings of a reply. For this reason, they can take the shape, as in the four letters included here, written between 24 January and 9 February 1813, of a slightly unsynchronized ongoing conversation: 'Friday Jany 29. I hope you received my little parcel … on Wednesday even^g … & that you will be ready to hear from me again on Sunday, for I feel that I must write to you to day.' Other letters are addressed to sailor brothers Frank and Charles and sent to naval stations as far afield as the Baltic and the West Indies; there are business letters to Austen's publisher John Murray and carefully worded acknowledgements of royal favour to James Stanier Clarke. In the next generation Aunt Jane was the confidante of nephew and nieces: Anna and Edward, the literary children of her eldest brother James, consulted their aunt about their novel writing; Fanny, brother Edward's daughter, moving in more fashionable circles at Godmersham, sought advice on her love life.

The originals of the letters are scattered worldwide in public and private collections. Of the thirteen letters presented here, twelve are now owned by Jane Austen's House Museum and one by the Jane Austen Society. Eleven were written by Jane Austen herself, one is in the hand of James Stanier Clarke and one in that of Cassandra Austen. Together they form a small but wonderful collection tracing a lively story beginning in 1801, when, aged twenty-five, Austen left Steventon, her home since childhood, to move to Bath on her father's retirement. Recorded here are insights into the Austens' social life in the busy early months in the city and, from 1809, the more settled relationships formed at Chawton. Other letters describe trips to London for shopping, theatres and exhibitions. The poem-letter of 1809 was drafted to send to Frank Austen in China; yet others enrich our knowledge of the writing, publishing and early reception of three of the novels: *Pride and Prejudice*, *Mansfield Park* and *Emma*. A final letter, from July 1817, was written days after Austen's death by her beloved sister Cassandra.

I have called the collection 'The Chawton Letters' because all thirteen have at last found a home in Jane Austen's former house in Chawton. Some were written by Jane from Chawton; others were addressed by Jane to Chawton. The title also registers the debt we owe Cassandra Austen, whose later years were spent in that same house in Chawton and who there

treasured her sister's manuscripts and letters until her own
death dispersed them.

HOW TO READ A LETTER

There is an art to reading, as there is to writing, a letter;
significant meaning lies outside the chief matter of its text.
Where was it written; how neatly or casually were the words
set down; how formally is its recipient addressed; is it in ink
or pencil or typed; how is its paper filled and folded; how was
it sent? As centuries-old protocols and routines for writing,
sending and receiving letters shift from practice into memory
or are abandoned and forgotten altogether, transformed and
replaced by a variety of electronic messaging technologies,
we are more keenly alert than ever to the power of the
handwritten (and even the typed) letter: above all, to how it
carries the trace of its writer. This is the case with original
documents, but even a printed copy will retain some of these
extra-textual features.

Jane Austen used a standard letter-writing paper, sold
over the stationer's counter in folded sheets or booklets of
four pages.[3] Four pages made up the basic letter format in
her day, with the main text of the letter covering pages one to
three and the upper and lower portions of page four, while the
middle portion of this final page was reserved for the address,
or 'direction' as it was then called, of the recipient. There were
no separate envelopes at this time; the letter was folded from
top and bottom, its ends tucked in and sealed with a wax wafer.

I do not mean however to put Mrs H. out of conceit with her Society; if she is satisfied - well:- if she thinks others satisfied -
still better;- I say nothing of the complaints which reach one
from all quarters. Tell poor Mrs Sclater if you like it, while
you are at Manydown. - Miss Benn dined here on friday, I
have not seen her since; there is still work for one evening
more. I know nothing of the Prowtings. The Clements are

at home & are reduced to read. They have got Miss Edgeworth. - I have disposed of Mrs Grant for the 2d fortnight
to Mrs Digweed; - it can make no difference to her, which
of the 26 fortnights in the Year, the 3 vol.s lay in her
House. It is raining furiously - & tho' only a storm, I shall
probably send my Letter to Alton instead of going, my:
:self. - I had no thoughts of your writing by Mr Gray.
On Sunday or Tuesday I suppose I shall hear. -
Cook does not think the Mead in a state to be stopped down

A local post for London had begun as a penny post in 1680; it became twopence in 1801, with letters picked up and delivered as many as eight times daily. Outside London, postage, based on weight and distance travelled, was paid by the recipient. Members of Parliament were allowed to send correspondence free of charge, 'franking' letters by writing the address (and, after 1784, the date) in their own hands, a privilege they would often extend to friends.

In general, though, the charge upon the recipient acted as an incentive for the writer to economize by using every scrap of paper: squeezing extra text between the lines and, on occasion, turning the completed page and writing at right angles across the text. A tidy hand and a thrifty way with paper were matters of pride, as Miss Bates attests in praising Jane Fairfax's skill in such things: 'in general she fills the whole

FACING The address panel of a letter from Jane Austen to Cassandra Austen, 9 February 1813 (Letter 7). Envelopes were not used in this period, letters consisting of a single sheet of paper, folded to make four pages. The creases show how the letter was finally tucked in on itself, with the middle section of the fourth page used as an address panel. To try it for yourself, take a piece of paper and fold it in half to form four pages (this is how your blank writing paper would look – though with different dimensions). Write your letter on the first three pages and the top and bottom third of the fourth page but leaving its middle section blank. Fold the bottom third up and the top third down so that the edges meet in the middle. Then, holding the letter lengthways, fold the left-hand and right-hand sides in and tuck one end into the other. Seal with wax and write the address on the reverse.

paper and crosses half' (*Emma*, ch. 19). Thrift, too, helps explain Jane Austen's much be-dashed writing style in these letters: some of her dashes mark a change of subject where we might expect to see a new paragraph; dashes are, of course, more economical of paper than new paragraphs. As one contemporary authority wrote:

> A dash is very often put, in crowded print, in order to save the room that would be lost by the breaks of distinct paragraphs. This is another matter. Here the dash comes after a *full point*. It is the using of it in the middle of a sentence against which I caution you.[4]

Even in print, the pages of these letters retain the impression of a vital continuous conversational stream of bits and pieces of news, views and gossip – a particular idiom that we recognize as Jane Austen's own.

Each of the letters printed here is freshly transcribed and prefaced by an introduction situating it within Austen's life, annotating its contents (people, places, topics, events and points of interest mentioned within it) and explaining its provenance and arrival into the Museum's collection. I have made no attempt to standardize Austen's distinctive spelling and punctuation. I have also let stand her abbreviations and her inconsistent capitalization of initial letters for common nouns occurring mid-sentence and for setting down the days of the week – 'Saturday', 'friday'. These features do not impede the reader's understanding; indeed, I would argue that they add a further dimension. In the early nineteenth century, even among educated writers, spelling continued to retain, like handwriting itself, a more expressive and individual stamp, and variations in the appearance of a word (whether spelling or capitalization) should not be viewed as incorrect. Here, in the intimate context of the domestic or personal letter, such variation conveys the impression of the individual voice, which we would hardly wish to erase.

By contrast, the long-tailed 's',[5] still in use in the handwriting of Austen's contemporaries (William Wordsworth and John Keats, for example), contributes nothing to meaning and merely impedes the modern reader's enjoyment; accordingly, it is not reproduced here. Austen's multi-length dashes, a regular feature of her handwriting, are all rendered as one length; her double inverted speech marks are made single in line with modern British usage; her use of underlining for emphasis is retained; so, too, her use of raised letters (as in 'even[g]', 'M[rs]'); words either struck through or inserted above the line are represented as such. The page breaks within each letter are noted in square brackets; italic print within square brackets is used to give further details that might help the reader reconstruct Austen's way of filling its pages. The aim is to give the reader as much of the flavour of the handwritten page as possible without rendering its presentation unnecessarily fussy or obscure.

NOTES

1   James Edward Austen-Leigh, *A Memoir of Jane Austen and Other Family Recollections*, ed. Kathryn Sutherland, Oxford University Press, Oxford, 2002, p. 141.

2   Austen-Leigh, *A Memoir*, p. 174.

3   Quarto half-sheet bifolia, forming four-page booklets, each leaf measuring 235 x 190 mm (approx.) with some variation.

4   William Cobbett, *A Grammar of the English Language, in a Series of Letters* (1819), 1823 edition, reissued Oxford University Press, Oxford, 2002, pp. 79–80.

5   The long 'ʃ', used in preference to the short 's' as the first 's' in double 's', as in 'kindneʃs', 'succeʃs', 'Suʃsex'.

Letters

My dear Cassandra:

For your letter from Kintbu[ry]
the compliments on my writing which [...]
turn you my best thanks. — I am very [...]
rive to Chilton; a very essential temporar[y]
resence must afford to Mrs Craven, an[d]
ill endeavour to make it a lasting o[ne]
those kind offices in favour of the you[ng]
hich you were both with-held in the
Harrison family by the mistaken ten[der]
heart of ours. — The Endymion came [...]
n Sunday, & I have sent Charles a s[...]
this day's post. — My adventures sin[ce]
you three days ago have been such as [...]
easily contain; I walked yesterday m[orning]
Mr Chamberlayne to Lyncombe & Be[...]
in the evening I drank tea with the [...]
Chamberlayne's pace was not quite so [...]
n this second trial as in the first;
more than I could keep up with, wit[hout]
for many, many yards together on a

Letter 1

This letter was written from Bath over two days, 26–27 May 1801, to Cassandra Austen, then on a visit to the Fowles, long-standing family friends living in Kintbury, Berkshire. The Fowle sons had been educated by JA's father, the Revd George Austen, at Steventon Rectory. Tom Fowle became engaged to Cassandra but died of yellow fever off St Domingo in February 1797. On his death he left his fiancée £1,000, which, invested, would have helped to give her a limited independence. The Austens (Revd and Mrs Austen and JA) had, by the end of May 1801, been in Bath only a few weeks, having moved there on the Revd Austen's retirement. As this letter makes clear, they were still looking for settled accommodation and in the meantime were staying with the Leigh Perrots, JA's uncle and aunt, at their home, 1 Paragon Buildings. Possible houses to rent are mentioned: No. 12 Green Park Buildings, with its wet kitchen; a north-west facing property on Seymour Street, which was presumably too gloomy. The Austens eventually took a lease on No. 4 Sydney Place.

The letter provides a rich and amusing evocation of social life in Bath immediately after the move from Steventon, the only home JA had known until then. She was now aged twenty-five and ready to take full advantage of Bath's amusements, though there are signs that she already found the daily round of visiting, tea drinking and conversation stifling: 'Another stupid party last night; perhaps if larger they might be less intolerable' (Wednesday, 13 May 1801). From the outset there were strains, especially in relations with her aunt Leigh Perrot, whom she found tiresome. There was also the matter of Mrs Leigh Perrot's notoriety: in 1799 she had been gaoled on a charge of shoplifting and, though eventually acquitted in 1800, the scandal must still have hung in the air a year later and affected the family's social standing in that gossip-hungry city.

Among those mentioned in the letter are Martha Lloyd, close friend of JA and Cassandra, who became a permanent part of the Austen women's household after the Revd Austen's death in 1805; Frank Austen, the elder of JA's sailor brothers (for whom see Letter 3, the poem-letter of 26 July 1809); and Elizabeth Heathcote, another lifelong friend. The intriguing references to Mr Evelyn and his 'very bewitching Phaeton' make us wish to know more: how far did JA encourage the flirtation she hints at between them; or was it no more than a story spun to amuse her sister? How did Mr Evelyn acquire his reputation for being dangerous ('I really beleive he is very harmless; people do not seem afraid of him here')? Did he use his flashy carriage, like the crudely predatory John Thorpe of *Northanger Abbey* (ch. 11), to attract and seduce young women? Or did he really drive out into the countryside just to collect food ('Groundsel') for his birds? JA imbues the brief sketch with tantalizing and comic possibilities. Unfortunately, however, we know no more: the Evelyns, introduced in a letter of 11 June 1799 as acquaintances of JA's brother Edward, leave no deeper trace.

This letter is significant for its mention of the gift of gold chains and topaz crosses bought for his sisters by Charles, the youngest of the Austen children, with his share of prize money from the capture of an enemy ship. Charles, a lieutenant on HMS *Endymion*, had been on patrol in the western Mediterranean. His gift later provided JA with the idea for the 'very pretty amber cross' that William Price (modelled on Charles) brought from Sicily for his sister Fanny in *Mansfield Park* (ch. 26). The crosses accompanied the letter as it descended through the Austen family and, in the 1920s, into the auction house. The letter and crosses were purchased in 1966 by Charles Beecher Hogan and presented by him to the Jane Austen Society in 1974.

The letter has the postmark: 'BATH'.

Pathetically: the word had a slightly different range of meaning for JA than for us, closer to 'earnestly' or 'with strong feeling'. No criticism is intended.

Now this, says my Master will be mighty dull: a reference to the eighteenth-century familiar letter-writer Hester Thrale Piozzi's way of describing her husband and his opinions in her *Letters to and from the late Samuel Johnson* (1788).

Phaeton: a sporty open carriage.

Troops to Egypt: reinforcements in the successful British Egyptian Campaign (1801–2) against Napoleon.

4th of June … fireworks: the celebrations for King George III's birthday.

My dear Cassandra

For your letter from Kintbury & for all the compliments on my writing which it contained, I now return you my best thanks.—I am very glad that Martha goes to Chilton; a very essential temporary comfort her presence must afford to M[rs] Craven, and I hope she will endeavour to make it a lasting one by exerting those kind offices in favour of the Young Man, from which you were both with-held in the case of the Harrison family by the mistaken tenderness of one part of ours.—The Endymion came into Portsmouth on sunday, & I have sent Charles a short letter by this day's post.— My adventures since I wrote to you three days ago have been such as the time would easily contain; I walked yesterday morning with M[rs] Chamberlayne to Lyncombe & Widcombe, and in the evening I drank tea with the Holders.—M[rs] Chamberlayne's pace was not quite so magnificent on this second trial as in the first; it was nothing more than I could keep up with, without effort; & for many, many Yards together on a raised narrow footpath I led the way.—The Walk was very beautiful [p. 2] as my companion agreed, whenever I made the observation—And so ends our friendship, for the Chamberlaynes leave Bath in a day or two.—Prepare likewise for the loss of Lady Fust, as you will lose before you find her.—My evening visit was by no means disagreable. M[rs] Lillingston came to engage M[rs] Holder's conversation, &

Miss Holder & I adjourned after tea into the inner Drawing room to look over Prints & talk pathetically. She is very unreserved & very fond of talking of her deceased brother & Sister, whose memories she cherishes with an Enthusiasm, which tho' perhaps a little affected, is not unpleasing.—She has an idea of your being remarkably lively; therefore get ready the proper selection of adverbs, & due scraps of Italian & French.—I must now pause to make some observation on Mrs Heathcote's having got a little Boy; I wish her well to wear it out—& shall proceed.—Frank writes me word that he is to be in London tomorrow; some money Negociation from which he hopes to derive advantage, hastens him from Kent, & will detain him a few days behind my father in Town.—I have seen the Miss Mapletons this morning; Marianne was buried yesterday, and I called without expecting to be let in, to enquire after them all.— [*p. 3*] On the servant's invitation however I sent in my name, & Jane & Christiana who were walking in the Garden came to me immediately, and I sat with them about ten minutes.—They looked pale & dejected, but were more composed than I had thought probable.—When I mentioned your coming here on Monday, they said that they should be very glad to see you.—We drink tea to night with Mrs Lysons;—Now this, says my Master will be mighty dull.—On friday we are to have another party, & a sett of new people to you.—The Bradshaws & Greaves's, all belonging to one another, and I hope the Pickfords.—Mrs Evelyn called very civilly on sunday, to tell us that Mr Evelyn had seen M^r

Philips the proprietor of N° 12 G. P. B. and that Mr Philips
was very willing to raise the kitchen floor;—but all this I fear
is fruitless—tho' the water may be kept out $_\wedge$ of sight, it cannot be
sent away, nor the ill effects of its' nearness be excluded.—I
have nothing more to say on the subject of Houses;—except
that we were mistaken as to the aspect of the one in Seymour
Street, which instead of being due west is North west.—I
assure you inspite of what I might chuse to insinuate in a
former letter, that I have seen very little of Mr Evelyn since my
coming here; I met him this morning for only the 4th time, & as
to my anecdote about Sidney Gardens, I made the [*p. 4*] most
of the Story because it came in to advantage, but in fact he
only asked me whether I were to be at Sidney Gardens in the
evening or not.—There is now something like an engagement
between us & the Phaeton, which to confess my frailty I have
a great desire to go out in;—whether it will come to anything
must remain with him.—I really beleive he is very harmless;
people do not seem afraid of him here, and he gets Groundsel
for his birds & all that.—My Aunt will never be easy till
she visits them;—she has been repeatedly trying to fancy a
necessity for it now on our accounts, but she meets with no
encouragement.—She ought to be particularly scrupulous in
such matters, & she says so herself—but nevertheless— — —
— — Well—I am come home from Mrs Lysons as yellow as I
went;—You cannot like your yellow gown half so well as I do,
nor a quarter neither. Mr Rice & Lucy are to be married, one
on the 9th & the other on the 10th of July.—Y^{rs} affec:^{ly} JA.

[*the letter continues on p. 1, written upside down between the lines, beginning five lines from the foot of the page and working towards the top*]

<u>Wednesday</u>.—I am just returned from my Airing in the very bewitching Phaeton & four, for which I was prepared by a note from Mr E. soon after breakfast: We went to the top of Kingsdown—& had a very pleasant drive: One pleasure succeeds another rapidly—. On my return I found your letter & a letter from Charles on the table. The contents of yours I suppose I need not repeat to you; to thank you for it will be enough.—I give Charles great credit for remembering my Uncle's direction, & he seems rather surprised at it himself.— He has received 30£ for his share of the privateer & expects 10£ more—but of what avail is it to take prizes if he lays out the produce in presents to his Sisters. He has being [*sic*] buying Gold chains & Topaze Crosses for us;—he must be well scolded.—The Endymion has already received orders for taking Troops to Egypt—which I should not like at all if I did not trust to Charles' being removed from her somehow or other before she sails. He knows nothing of his own destination he says,—but desires me to write directly as the Endymion will probably sail in 3 or 4 days.—He will receive my yesterday's letter today, and I shall ~~probably~~ write again by this post to thank & reproach him.—We shall be unbearably fine.—I have made an engagement for you for Thursday the 4th of June; if my Mother & Aunt should not go to the fireworks,

which I dare say they will not, I have promised to join M^r
Evelyn & Miss Wood—. Miss Wood has lived with them you
know ever 'since my Son died—'.

[*postscript written below the address panel on p. 4*]
I will engage Mrs Mussell as you desire. She made my
dark gown very well & may therefore be trusted I hope
with Yours—but she does not always succeed with lighter
Colours—. My white one I was obliged to alter a good deal.—
Unless anything particular occurs, I shall not write again.

[*address panel reads*]
Miss Austen
The Rev:^d F. C. Fowle's
Kintbury
Newbury

Cambrick! with grateful blessings would I pa[y]
The pleasure given me in sweet employ
Long may'st thou serve my Friend without de[cay]
And have no tears to wipe, but tears of j[oy]

I A. — Aug.t 26. — 10[?]

That &c

Letter 2

INTRODUCTION

A poem-letter, it is addressed to Catherine Bigg, a close friend
of the Austens and sister of Elizabeth Heathcote (the birth of
whose son is mentioned in Letter 1, of 26 May 1801) and of
Harris Bigg-Wither, to whom JA was briefly (one night only
in December 1802) engaged to be married. The poem is dated
26 August 1808 and was sent with a gift of handkerchiefs.
JA was a skilled needlewoman; in January 1792 she had sent
a poem inside a 'housewife' (sewing kit) to Mary Lloyd.
In October 1808 Catherine married the Revd Herbert Hill,
uncle of the poet Robert Southey, and settled in Streatham,
then a village and now part of south London. JA expressed
reservations about the marriage to Cassandra in a letter of 24
October: Catherine was in her early thirties (JA's own age) and
Hill almost sixty.

The poem-letter was purchased by T. Edward Carpenter
at a Sotheby's sale on 8 July 1959 (lot 816) and bequeathed
by him to Jane Austen's House Museum in 1969. There is
another, longer version of the same poem, not sent, now in the
Fondation Martin Bodmer, Geneva.

Cambrick: a fine white linen cloth also used for making shirts. It was originally made in Cambrai, France.

Cambrick! with grateful blessings would I pay
    The pleasure given me in sweet employ:—
Long may'st thou serve my Friend without decay,
    And have no tears to wipe, but tears of joy!—
                JA.—Aug:ˢᵗ 26.—1808—

[*address on the other side reads*] Miss Bigg

My dearest Frank, I wish you joy
Of Mary's safety with a boy,
Whose birth has given little pain,
Compared with that of Mary Jane. —
May he a growing Blessing prove,
And well deserve his Parents' Love!
Endow'd with Art's & Nature's Good,
Thy name possessing with thy Blood,
In him, in all his ways, may we
Another Francis William see! —
Thy infant days may he inherit,
Thy warmth, nay insolence of spirit
We would not with one fault dispense
To weaken the resemblance.
May he revive thy Nursery sin,
Peeping as daringly within,
"His curley Locks but just descried,"
With, "Bet, my be not come to bide" —
Fearless of danger, braving pain,
And threaten'd very oft in vain,
Still may one Terror daunt his soul,
One needful engine of controul.
Be found in this sublime array,
A neighbouring Donkey's awful Bray
So may his equal faults as Child,

Letter 3

INTRODUCTION

Dated 26 July 1809, this is a draft copy in JA's own hand of
a poem-letter sent to brother Frank, on naval duty in China,
announcing the birth of his first son Francis William on 12
July and sharing another important piece of news: the Austen
women at last have a home of their own. We glimpse in the
poem's closing lines the cottage in Chawton, Hampshire,
into which, with their lifelong friend Martha Lloyd, they had
moved as recently as 7 July 1809, marking an end to years
of domestic insecurity. The women had first moved from
Bath to Southampton where, in October 1806, they shared
lodgings with Frank and his new wife. The offer of a cottage
on brother Edward's Hampshire estate only came in 1808 after
the death of Edward's wife. JA described Chawton Cottage's
'six Bedchambers' and 'Garrets for Storeplaces' in a letter to
Cassandra, 20 November 1808. Now, in possession of her
new home, she cannot hide her pleasure at the prospect it
affords for comfort and stability: 'when complete, | It will all
other Houses beat'. Frank's interest in the smallest detail of
their new arrangements could be guaranteed: living with his
mother and sisters in Southampton, he had busied himself
'making very nice fringe for the Drawingroom-Curtains'

(JA to Cassandra, 20-22 February 1807). The birth of his son also prompts, in the reference to Frank's own childhood naughtiness, a rare insight into the Austens' early family life.

Significantly, JA's verse letter is in the same metrical form as Walter Scott's bestselling romance *Marmion*, published the previous year. She had sent Frank a copy of Scott's poem a few months previously for him to pass on to their brother Charles (as she reported in a letter of 10–11 January 1809 to Cassandra), giving more point to the use here of its borrowed form. JA wrote light, often comic, verses throughout her life to amuse her family.

The poem, as posted to Frank, is now in the British Library, London; JA's draft copy was bought by T. Edward Carpenter for £70 in May/June 1956 from Rosemary Mowll, Frank Austen's great-granddaughter, and bequeathed by him to Jane Austen's House Museum in 1969.

'*Bet, my be not come to bide*': JA is reminding Frank of his own baby talk. After their first few months, all the Austen children were handed over to a village woman for the next year or longer, certainly until able to walk. Such nursing out was not uncommon in the late eighteenth century when gentry women like Mrs Austen combined large families with other responsibilities. The Austen parents are said to have visited their babies daily. Deirdre Le Faye has suggested that a couple called John and Elizabeth Littleworth may have been regular foster-parents to the Austen children and that their daughter, Bet, was their nursemaid and playfellow ('The Austens and the Littleworths', Jane Austen Society Report, 1987, pp. 64–70).

over-right us: that is, staying only half a mile away in Chawton House, Edward's manor house on his Chawton estate, which became a temporary home to the Austen brothers when they visited.

Copy of a letter to Frank, July 26, 1809.

My dearest Frank, I wish you Joy
Of Mary's safety with a boy,
Whose birth has given little pain,
Compared with that of Mary Jane.—
May he a growing Blessing prove,
And well deserve his Parents Love!
Endow'd with Art's & Nature's Good,
Thy name possessing with thy Blood,
In him, in all his ways, may we
Another Francis William see!—
Thy infant days may he inherit,
Thy warmth, nay insolence of spirit;—
We would not with one fault dispense
To weaken the resemblance.
May he revive thy Nursery sin,
Peeping as daringly within,
(His curley Locks but just descried)
With, 'Bet, my be not come to bide.'
Fearless of danger, braving pain,
And threaten'd very oft in vain,
Still may one Terror daunt his soul
One needful engine of controul
Be found in this sublime array,
A neigbouring [*sic*] Donkey's aweful Bray!—
So may his equal faults as Child

Produce Maturity as mild,
His saucy words & fiery ways
In early Childhood's pettish days
[*p. 2*] In Manhood shew his Father's mind,
Like him considerate & kind;
All Gentleness to those around,
And eager only not to wound.
Then like his Father too, he must,
To his own former struggles just,
Feel his Deserts with honest Glow,
And all his Self-improvement know.—
A native fault may thus give birth
To the best blessing, conscious worth.—

    As for ourselves, we're very well,
As unaffected prose will tell.
Cassandra's pen will give our state
The many comforts that await
Our Chawton home—how much we find
Already in it to our mind,
And how convinced that when complete,
It will all other Houses beat,
That ever have been made or mended,
With rooms concise or rooms distended.

    You'll find us very snug next year;
Perhaps with Charles & Fanny near—
For now it often does delight us
To fancy them just over-right us.

                 J. A.

My dear Cassandra.

This is exactly the weather
you are, but well enough to enjoy it. I [...]
[y]ou are not confined to the house by an [...]
weed has used us barely. Handsome is a [...]
therefore a very ill looking Man. I hope [...]
letter to me by this day's post, unless yo[u]
[w]ill tomorrow by one of Mr Chutes franks.
[s]ince you went away, & no visitor, except
with us on friday; but we have received
[s]tilton cheese — we presume, from Henry.
[...]well & finds great amusement in the g[...]
hair is finished, she means to knit another,
[o]ther work. — We quite run over with [...]
John Carr's Travels in Spain from Miss [...]
[S]ociety — Octavo, an Essay on the Military [...]
British Empire, by Capt. Pasley of the E[...]
I protested against at first, but which i[s]
[de]lightfully written & highly entertaining,
with the Author as I ever was with Clar[e]
even the two Mr Smiths of the city. The
[s]ighed for; but he does write with all [...]
[Y]esterday moreover brought us Mrs Gra[...]
[W]hites Compts — But I have disposed of [...]

Letter 4

This is the first in a group of four letters written by JA from Chawton in January and February 1813 to Cassandra Austen who was staying elsewhere in Hampshire: first at Steventon Rectory (24 January–4 February) with their eldest brother James and his family; later at Manydown (9 February), home of their friends, the Bigg sisters. An unbroken group, these letters allow us to hear JA's side of a continuing conversation filled with observations on Chawton neighbours and their doings, the success of the local Alton Book Society and, from 29 January, rare details of the publication and early reception of *Pride and Prejudice*, as well as anxious moments of self-criticism as she finally sees her novel in print. Of interest, too, are the particulars shared with Cassandra (her regular confidante) on the progress of a new novel, *Mansfield Park*.

We hear those 'little matters' (see my Introduction), everyday circumstances that leap off the page and bring JA's world to life with surprising freshness: brother Henry's gift of half a Stilton cheese; the instruction to Mary Austen at Steventon that her mother-in-law's declared preference is for pork 'from the two *last* Pigs'; reports of headaches and colds. A rich sense of local community and of the leading features of particular individuals builds across all four letters, inevitably drawing comparison in the reader's mind with the preoccupations of the small town society of *Emma*. In these Chawton letters we meet 'my own dear Thomas' (Thomas Carter, manservant at Chawton Cottage); Miss Benn, a Miss Bates-like spinster living in poor circumstances and, in consequence, the recipient of regular charitable dinners at neighbours' houses; the Digweeds, the Papillons (rector of Chawton and his sister), the Prowtings and, from further afield, various members of the Terry family of Dummer, Hampshire, around 20 miles distance from Chawton; among them is 'Miss P. T.' (Patience Terry) who may or may not be receiving the attentions of 'Mᵣ P.' (Revd Papillon?), and 'brother Michael' (Terry).

This first letter was, at a later date, marked at the top of p. 1 with 'I', presumably to link it to the next three, each of which is also numbered. Though begun on Sunday, 24 January, JA was still writing it the following Tuesday, weaving into the final page immediate news and responses to items in Cassandra's latest letter, received that day.

All four letters descended through Charles Austen's branch of the family and were sold by his granddaughters in the 1920s. All four were bought, following the Sotheby sale of May 1948, by T. Edward Carpenter, and bequeathed by him to Jane Austen's House Museum in 1969. Carpenter's purchase price for this first letter in the group of four was £100.

Mʳ Chute's franks: William John Chute, who, as Member of Parliament for Hampshire, could frank letters, allowing them to be posted free of charge.

Sir John Carr's Travels … Capt. Pasley of the Engineers: *Descriptive Travels in the Southern and Eastern Parts of Spain and the Balearic Isles, in the year 1809* (1811), by Sir John Carr, KC, a popular travel writer; *Essay on the Military Policy and Institutions of the British Empire* (1810), by Charles Pasley, Captain in the Royal Engineers. Both books show the strong influence of the ongoing Napoleonic Wars on JA's reading taste. She returned to praise Pasley elsewhere in her letters. No doubt she enjoyed his plain style and dry wit, not to mention his unreserved praise for the British navy—explanation enough for her comment later in this letter that he is '[t]he first soldier I ever sighed for', echoing the words of Miranda in Shakespeare's *The Tempest*, I. ii: 'This | Is the third man that e'er I saw; the first | That e'er I sigh'd for.' As explained a few lines later in this letter, Carr's book allowed JA to correct a mistake in *Mansfield Park*, the novel she was currently writing, where she had William Price visiting Government House (now corrected to 'the Commissioner's') in Gibraltar (ch. 24).

Society-Octavo: octavo is a common format or size for a new book; 'Society' refers to the Alton Book Society through which the Austens and their neighbours enjoyed the loan of the various volumes.

Clarkson … the two Mr Smiths: a surprisingly diverse list of authors and books. Thomas Clarkson, *The History of the Rise, Progress, and Accomplishment of the Abolition of the African Slave-Trade by the British Parliament* (1808), was another work turned to good use in *Mansfield Park* (ch. 21), where Fanny Price questions her uncle, newly returned from his plantations in Antigua, 'about the slave trade'. Claudius Buchanan, *Christian Researches in Asia* (1811), is an account of travels in south and west India and of the author's attempt to organize systematic translations of the Christian scriptures. James Smith and his brother Horatio produced the popular *Rejected Addresses; or, The New Theatrum Poetarum* (1812), a collection of parodies of contemporary poets.

Mrs Grants Letters: Anne Grant, *Letters from the Mountains; being the real correspondence of a Lady, between the years 1773 and 1803* (1806).

Tax-cart: more correctly 'taxed' cart; an open horse-drawn cart used for farm or trade purposes, on which there was a reduced duty.

their round Table … Mrs Grants: another reference to *Mansfield Park* (ch. 25), where the 'remaining six' form a round game of Speculation after the four players needed for whist have set up their table.

Biglands … & Mackenzies: John Bigland, *A Geographical and Historical View of the World* (1810); John Barrow, *Travels in China* (1804); George, Lord Macartney's *Journal of the Embassy to China* appeared in a second volume of Barrow's work, *Some Account of the Public Life, and a Selection from the Unpublished Writings of the Earl of Macartney* (1807); Sir George Steuart Mackenzie, *Travels in the Island of Iceland* (1812). Here is yet another link to *Mansfield Park*, where Macartney on China is amongst Fanny Price's reading (ch. 16).

something in a Cover: as an extra sheet, this would have doubled the charge of the letter to the recipient. Le Faye suggests that this letter, with its extra material (in response to Cassandra's letter that arrived during the course of its writing), may have been sent inside the parcel collected from Alton by John Bond (see Letter 5 and *Jane Austen's Letters*, ed. Deirdre Le Faye, 4th edition, Oxford University Press, Oxford, 2011, p. 419 note 15). There is no evidence to suggest that the letter went through the post in the usual way.

Martha … under her bed: a reference to the other resident of Chawton Cottage, Martha Lloyd, who is also away at this time; the 'rogues' are probably the Cottage dogs.

Letter to Anna: Anna Austen, eldest child of James Austen, one of JA's favourite nieces and her collaborator from early childhood in writing fictions for family entertainment.

Poor Charles & his frigate: a reference to JA's youngest brother, Charles, at the time commanding HMS *Namur* on harbour service in the Thames Estuary. He was given the command of the 36-gun frigate HMS *Phoenix* in September 1814.

My dear Cassandra

    This is exactly the weather we could wish for, if you are but well enough to enjoy it. I shall be glad to hear that you are not confined to the house by an increase of Cold. Mr Digweed has used us basely. Handsome is as Handsome does; he is therefore a very ill-looking Man. I hope you have sent off a Letter to me by this day's post, unless you are tempted to wait till tomorrow by one of Mr Chute's franks.—We have had no letter since you went away, & no visitor, except Miss Benn who dined with us on friday; but we have received the half of an excellent Stilton cheese—we presume, from Henry.—My Mother is very well & finds great amusement in the glove-knitting; when this pair is finished, she means to knit another, & at present wants no other work.—We quite run over with Books. <u>She</u> has got Sir John Carr's Travels in Spain from Miss B. & <u>I</u> am reading a Society-Octavo, an Essay on the Military Police & Institutions of the British Empire, by Capt. Pasley of the Engineers, a book which I protested against at first, but which upon trial I find delightfully written & highly entertaining. I am as much in love with the Author as I ever was with Clarkson or Buchanan, or even the two Mr Smiths of the city. The first soldier I ever sighed for; but he does write with extraordinary force & spirit. Yesterday moreover brought us Mrs Grants Letters, with Mr White's Comp^{ts}—But I have disposed of them, Comp^ts & all, for the first fortnight to Miss Papillon—& among so many readers or retainers of Books as we have in Chawton, I dare say there will [*p. 2*] be no difficulty in getting rid of them for another fortnight if necessary.— I learn from Sir J. Carr that there is no Government House at Gibraltar.—I must alter it to the Commissioner's.—Our party on Wednesday was not unagreeable, tho' as usual we wanted a better Master of the House, one less anxious & fidgetty, & more conversible. In consequence of a civil note that morn^g from Mrs Clement, I went with her & her Husband in their Tax-cart;—civility on both sides; I would rather have walked, & no doubt, they must have wished I had.—I ran home with my own dear Thomas at night in great Luxury. Thomas was so very useful.—We were Eleven altogether, as you will find on computation, adding Miss Benn & two strange Gentlemen, a Mr Twyford, curate of G^t Worldham who is living in Alton, & his friend Mr Wilkes.—I do not know that Mr T. is anything, except very dark-complexioned, but Mr W. was a useful addition, being an easy, talking, pleasantish young Man;—a very young Man, hardly 20 perhaps. He is of St Johns, Cambridge, & spoke very highly of H. Walter as a Schollar;—he said he was considered as the best Classick in the University.—How, such a report would have interested my Father!—I could see nothing very promising between Mr P. & Miss P. T.—She placed herself on one side of him at first, but Miss Benn obliged her to move up higher;—& she had an empty plate, & even asked him to give her some

Mutton without being attended to for some time.—There might be Design in this, to be sure, on his side;—he might think an empty Stomach the most favourable for Love.—Upon Mrs Digweed's mentioning that she had sent the Rejected Addresses to Mr Hinton, I began talking to her a little about them & expressed my hope of their having amused her. Her answer was, 'Oh! dear, [*p. 3*] yes, very much;—very droll indeed;—the opening of the House!—& the striking up of the Fiddles!'—What she meant, poor Woman, who shall say?— I sought no farther.—The Papillons have now got the Book & like it very much;—their neice Eleanor has recommended it most warmly to them.—<u>She</u> looks like a rejected Addresser. As soon as a Whist party was formed & a round Table threatened, I made my Mother an excuse, & came away; leaving just as many for <u>their</u> round Table, as there were at Mrs Grants.—I wish they might be as agreable a set.—It was past 10 when I got home, so I was not ashamed of my dutiful Delicacy.—The Coulthards were talked of you may be sure; no end of <u>them</u>; Miss Terry had heard they were going to rent Mr Bramston's house at Oakley, & Mrs Clement that they were going to live at Streatham.—Mrs Digweed & I agreed that the House at Oakley could not possibly be large enough for them, & now we find they have really taken it.—Mr Gauntlett is thought very agreable, & there are <u>no</u> Children at all.— The Miss Sibleys want to establish a Book society in their side of the Country, like ours. What can be a stronger proof of that superiority in ours over the Steventon & Manydown Society, which I have always foreseen & felt?—No emulation of the kind was ever inspired by their proceedings; no such wish of the Miss Sibleys was ever heard, in the course of the many years of that Society's existence;—And what are their Biglands & their Barrows, their Macartneys & Mackenzies, to Capt. Pasley's Essay on the Military Police of the British Empire, & the rejected Addresses? I have walked once to Alton, & yesterday Miss Papillon & I walked together to call on the Garnets. She invited herself very pleasantly to be my companion, when I went to propose to her the indulgence of accomodating us about the Letters from the Mountains. I had a very agreable walk; if she had not, more shame for her, for I was quite as entertaining as she was. Dame G. is pretty well, & we found her surrounded by her well-behaved, healthy, large-eyed Children.—I took her an old Shift & promised her a set of our Linen; & my Companion left some of her Bank Stock with her. [*p. 4*] Tuesday has done its duty, & I have had the pleasure of reading a very comfortable Letter. It contains so much, that I feel obliged to write down the whole of this page & perhaps something in a Cover.—When my parcel is finished I shall walk with it to Alton. I beleive Miss Benn will go with me. She spent yesterday evening with us.—As I know Mary is interested in her not being neglected by her neighbours, pray tell her that Miss B. dined last wednesday at Mr Papillons—on Thursday with Capt. & Mrs Clement—friday here—saturday with Mrs Digweed—& Sunday with the Papillons again.—I had fancied that Martha w^d be at Barton from last saturday, but am best pleased to be mistaken. I hope she is now quite well.—Tell her that I hunt away the rogues every night from under her bed; they feel the difference of her being gone.—Miss Benn wore her new shawl last night, sat in it the whole even^g & seemed to enjoy it very much.—'A very sloppy Lane' last friday!—What an odd sort of country you must be in! I cannot at all understand it! It was just greasy here on friday, in consequence of the little snow that had fallen in the night.—Perhaps it <u>was</u> cold on Wednesday, yes, I beleive it certainly was—but nothing terrible.—Upon the whole, the Weather for Winter-weather is delightful, the walking excellent.—I cannot imagine what sort of a place Steventon can be!—My Mother sends her Love to Mary, with Thanks for her kind intentions & enquiries as to the Pork, & will prefer receiving her Share from the two <u>last</u> Pigs.—She has great pleasure in sending her a pair of Garters, & is very glad that she had them ready knit.—Her Letter to Anna is to be forwarded, if any opportunity offers; otherwise it may wait for her return.—Mrs Leigh's Letter came this morn^g—We are glad to hear any thing so tolerable of Scarlets.—Poor Charles & his frigate. But there could be no chance of his having one, while it was thought such a certainty.—I can hardly beleive brother Michael's news; we have no such idea in Chawton at least.— Mrs Bramstone is the sort of Woman I detest.—Mr Cottrell is worth ten of her. It is better to be given the Lie direct, than to excite no interest. [*end of p. 4, last leaf of the letter is missing*]

I hope you received my little parcel b
day even[g], my dear Cassandra, & that you will
e again on Sunday, for I feel that I must w
your parcel is safely arrived & everything shall
thank you for your note. As you had not hea
time. it was very good in you to write, but
our debtor soon. I want to tell you that I
aking child from London; on wednesday I re
own by Falknor, with three lines from Henr
iven another to Charles & sent a 3d by the
first the two Setts which I was least eager fo
I wrote to him immediately to beg for one b
e would take the trouble of forwarding the
renton & Portsmouth — not having an idea
afore to day; — by your account however he w
etter was written. The only evil is the Dela
an be done till his return. Tell James &
love. — For your sake I am as well pleased
s it might be unpleasant to you to be in
t the first burst of the business. — The Adve
aper to day for the first time; — 18. — It
ny two neat, & £1.8 — for my stupides
rite to Frank, that he may not think h
Miss Benn dined with us on the very da
ing, & in the even[g] we set fairly at it &
o her — prefacing that having intelligence f
uch a work w[d] soon appear we had desi
.........it came out — & I believe it pass

Letter 5

INTRODUCTION

This letter, written 29 January 1813, is marked at the top of p. 1 with the number '2', being the second in the series written to Cassandra Austen from Chawton in early 1813. Its chief matter is the arrival in Hampshire of the first copies of *Pride and Prejudice* (published 28 January) from its London publisher, Thomas Egerton, and the secrecy over her authorship that JA wished to be maintained outside her immediate family. The novel's title page simply read: 'by the Author of *Sense and Sensibility*'. Carpenter paid £120 for this second letter in the group of four.

my own darling Child: JA referred elsewhere to her novels as her children, writing in late 1815 or early 1816 to her niece Anna, whose new daughter she had not yet seen: 'As I wish very much to see *your* Jemima, I am sure you will like to see *my* Emma' (*Jane Austen's Letters*, ed. Le Faye, p. 323).

18ˢ … my stupidest of all: *Pride and Prejudice* (in three volumes) went on sale at 18 shillings. 'He shall ask' refers to brother Henry Austen, who acted as JA's informal agent over publishing matters. The remark suggests JA's mounting confidence as professional writer and determination to profit financially from her talent. In the event, the next two novels, *Mansfield Park* and *Emma*, sold for 18 shillings and 21 shillings (that is, £1 1s.) respectively. It is not certain which novel JA meant by 'my stupidest of all': it cannot be *Emma*, as Le Faye suggests (*Jane Austen's Letters*, ed. Le Faye, p. 420), as, according to Cassandra Austen, it was not begun before January 1814.

Elizabeth: Elizabeth Bennet, heroine of *Pride and Prejudice*.

Typical errors: errors of typography or printing.

Two such people: JA and her mother, who were reading the novel aloud.

'I do not … Ingenuity themselves': an echo or appropriation of lines from Walter Scott's *Marmion* (1808): 'I do not rhyme to that dull elf, | Who cannot image to himself' (canto 6, stanza 38).

lopt & cropt: the novel was a revised version of an earlier manuscript, entitled 'First Impressions' (mentioned in a letter to Cassandra, 8–9 January 1799), but since no manuscripts survive it is impossible to tell how heavily JA pruned and altered it.

Ordination … Country of Hedgerows: further evidence (see Letter 4) that JA is deep in writing *Mansfield Park*. Cassandra is visiting their clergyman brother James at Steventon Rectory, where she has presumably been gleaning information about the process of ordination, to be used in the portrayal of Edmund Bertram (ch. 26). JA now sets her to find out about hedgerows, perhaps to confirm details used in ch. 22, where Fanny Price muses upon 'a rough hedgerow'.

your Charades: the whole Austen family enjoyed playing and composing riddles and word games. Two of Cassandra's charades are reprinted in David Selwyn (ed.), *Collected Poems and Verse of the Austen Family*, Fyfield Books, Manchester, 1996.

Betsy: maidservant at Chawton Cottage.

Miss Caroline: James Austen's youngest child, at the time aged seven.

Chawton, Friday Jany 29.

I hope you received my little parcel by J. Bond on
Wednesday even^g, my dear Cassandra, & that you will be ready
to hear from me again on Sunday, for I feel that I must write to
you to day. Your parcel is safely arrived & everything shall be
delivered as it ought. Thank you for your note. As you had not
heard from me at that time it was very good in you to write,
but I shall not be so much your debtor soon.—I want to tell
you that I have got my own darling Child from London;—
on wednesday I received one Copy, sent down by Falknor,
with three lines from Henry to say that he had given another
to Charles & sent a 3^d by the Coach to Godmersham; just the
two Sets which I was least eager for the disposal of. I wrote to
him immediately to beg for my two other Sets, unless he would
take the trouble of forwarding them at once to Steventon &
Portsmouth—not having an idea of his leaving Town before to
day;—by your account however he was gone before my Letter
was written. The only evil is the delay, nothing more can be
done till his return. Tell James & Mary so, with my Love.—
For <u>your</u> sake I am as well pleased that it sh^d be so, as it might
be unpleasant to you to be in the Neighbourhood at the first
burst of the business.—The Advertisement is in our paper
today for the first time;—<u>18</u>^{s}—He shall ask £1-1- for my two
next, & £1-8- for my stupidest of all.—I shall write to Frank,
that he may not think himself neglected. Miss Benn dined with
us on the very day of the Books coming, & in the even^g we set

fairly at it & read half the 1st vol. to her—prefacing that having intelligence from Henry that such a work wd soon appear we had desired him to send it whenever it came out—& I beleive it passed with her unsuspected.—She was [*p. 2*] amused, poor soul! that she cd not help you know, with two such people to lead the way; but she really does seem to admire Elizabeth. I must confess that I think her as delightful a creature as ever appeared in print, & how I shall be able to tolerate those who do not like her at least, I do not know.—There are a few Typical errors—& a 'said he' or a 'said she' would sometimes make the Dialogue more immediately clear—but 'I do not write for such dull Elves'

'As have not a great deal of Ingenuity themselves.'— The 2d vol. is shorter than I cd wish—but the difference is not so much in reality as in look, there being a larger proportion of Narrative in that part. I have lopt & cropt so successfully however that I imagine it must be rather shorter than S & S. altogether.—Now I will try to write of something else;—it shall be a complete change of subject—Ordination. I am glad to find your enquiries have ended so well.—If you cd discover whether Northamptonshire is a Country of Hedgerows, I shd be glad again.—We admire your Charades excessively, but as yet have guessed only the 1st. The others seem very difficult. There is so much beauty in the versification however, that the finding them out is but a secondary pleasure.—I grant you that this is a cold day, & am sorry to think how cold you will be through the process of your visit at Manydown. I hope you will wear your China Crape. Poor wretch! I can see you shivering away, with your miserable feeling feet.—What a vile Character Mr Digweed turns out; quite beyond anything & everything;—instead of going to Steventon they are to have a Dinnerparty next tuesday!—I am sorry to say that I could not eat a Mincepie at Mr Papillon's; I was rather head-achey that day, & c^d not venture on anything sweet except Jelly; but <u>that</u> was excellent.—There were no stewed pears; but Miss Benn had some almonds & raisins.—By the bye, she desired to be kindly remembered to you when I wrote last, & I forgot it.—Betsy sends her Duty to you & hopes you are well, & her Love to Miss Caroline & hopes she has got rid of her Cough. It was such a pleasure to her to think her Oranges were so well timed, that I dare say she was rather glad to hear of the Cough. [*end of p. 2*]

[*the second leaf of the letter is missing but there is a concluding postscript written upside down at the top of p. 1*]

Since I wrote this Letter we have been visited by Mrs Digweed, her Sister & Miss Benn. I gave Mrs D. her little parcel, which she opened here & seemed much pleased with—& $_{\wedge}$^{she} desired me to make her best Thanks &c. to Miss Lloyd for it.— — Martha may guess how full of wonder & gratitude she was.

My dear Cassandra

Your letter was truly welcom[e]
you all for your praise; it came at a right
me fits of disgust; — our 2d evening's reading to
e so well, but I believe something must be d
s rapid way of getting on — & tho' she perfectly
es herself, she cannot speak as they ought. — Up
am quite vain enough & well satisfied enough
s light & bright & sparkling; — it wants shade; — it
t here & there with a long Chapter — of sense if
solemn specious nonsense — about something unc
e Essay on Writing, a critique on Walter Scott, o
arte — or anything that would form a contrast
increase delight to the playfulness & Epigramma
le. — I doubt your quite agreeing with me here
otions. — The Caution observed at Steventon with
the Books is an agreable surprise to me, &
the means of saving you from everything
ust be prepared for the Neighbourhood being
loured of there being such a work in the Co
orld! — Dummer will do that you know.
e morn!, when Mrs D. called with Miss B
u in the Printing that I have met with is
here two speeches are made into one. — The
ave been no Suppers at Longbourn, bet
emains of Mrs Bennet's old Meryton ha
own disappointment about Manydown, & j

Letter 6

INTRODUCTION

Marked at the top of p. 1 with the number '3', this is the third letter, written 4 February, in the series to Cassandra Austen from Chawton in early 1813. The comments, much quoted by Austen critics and biographers, on the light, playful wit of *Pride and Prejudice*, gain significance from their context within a group of letters in which the novel then preoccupying JA's thoughts looms so large—the altogether more sombre and moralizing *Mansfield Park*. The purchase price for this the third letter in the group of four was £110.

every thing unpleasant: evidence of JA's concern to keep her authorship a secret from all but family and close friends.

Dummer: the home of the Terry family, introduced in the letter of 24 January 1813 (Letter 4). JA clearly thinks them indiscreet over the secret of her authorship.

Old Meryton habits: not only does JA notice the printer's mistake in *Pride and Prejudice* where two speeches were run together ('How hard it is …' 'And how impossible …' at the close of ch. 54 in any modern edition), she also appears critical of her reference, in the same chapter, to Mrs Bennet's wish to serve supper. Since the time when the novel was first drafted in the 1790s, supper had become unfashionable, and dinner, the main meal, moved to later in the day.

Crape … Bombasin: silk or woollen fabrics; both were associated with mourning garments.

the Harwoods: a local Hampshire family, living near Steventon, left ruined when the death of its head, John Harwood, in January 1813, revealed huge debts. It meant that the son and heir, another John Harwood, was unable to marry JA's widowed friend Elizabeth Bigg Heathcote (see Letter 7, 9 February 1813).

Thomas: the Austens' manservant, Thomas Carter, married Ann Trimmer on 30 January 1813. He was replaced by Browning.

Edward: JA's third brother, Edward Austen, who took the surname 'Knight' (from his adopted parents) in 1812. He was owner of estates at Godmersham, Kent, and Chawton.

copies … to S & P: of *Pride and Prejudice*, sent to Steventon and Portsmouth (to Frank Austen).

Adlestrop: a village in Gloucestershire, the home of JA's mother's family, the Leighs, since the sixteenth century.

My dear Cassandra

Your letter was truely welcome & I am much obliged to you all for your praise; it came at a right time, for I had had some fits of disgust;—our 2^d evening's reading to Miss Benn had not pleased me so well, but I beleive something must be attributed to my Mother's too rapid way of getting on—& tho' she perfectly understands the Characters herself, she cannot speak as they ought.—Upon the whole however I am quite vain enough & well satisfied enough.—The work is rather too light & bright & sparkling;—it wants shade;—it wants to be stretched out here & there with a long Chapter—of sense if it could be had, if not of solemn specious nonsense—about something unconnected with the story; an Essay on Writing, a critique on Walter Scott, or the history of Buonaparté—or anything that would form a contrast & bring the reader with increased delight to the playfulness & Epigrammatism of the general stile.—I doubt your quite agreeing with me here.— I know your starched Notions.—The caution observed at Steventon with regard to the possession of the Book is an agreable surprise to me, & I heartily wish it may be the means of saving you from every thing unpleasant;—but you must be prepared for the Neighbourhood being perhaps already informed of there being such a work in the World, & in the Chawton World! Dummer will do that you know.—It was spoken of here one morn^g when Mrs D. called with Miss

Benn.—The greatest blunder in the Printing that I have met with is in Page 220—Vol. 3. where two speeches are made into one.—There might as well have been no suppers at Longbourn, but I suppose it was the remains of Mrs Bennet's old Meryton habits.—I am sorry for your disappointment about Manydown, & fear this week must be a heavy one. As far as one may venture to judge at a distance of 20 miles [*p. 2*] you must miss Martha. For <u>her</u> sake I was glad to hear of her going, as I suppose she must have been growing anxious, & wanting to be again in scenes of agitation & exertion.— She had a lovely day for her journey. I walked to Alton, & dirt excepted, found it delightful,—it seemed like an old Feby. come back again.—Before I set out we were visited by Mrs Edwards, & while I was gone Miss Beckford & Maria, & Miss Woolls & Harriet B. called, all of whom my Mother was glad to see & I very glad to escape.—John M. is sailed, & now Miss B. thinks his Father will really try for a house, & has hopes herself of avoiding Southampton;—this is, as it was repeated to me;—and I can tell the Miss Williamses that Miss Beckford has no intention of inviting them to Chawton.—Well done You.—I thought of you at Manydown in the Draw^{g} room & in your China Crape;—therefore, you were in the Breakfast parlour in your Brown Bombasin;—if I thought of you <u>so</u>, you would have been in the Kitchen in your Morning stuff.— I feel that I have never mentioned the Harwoods in my Letters to you, which is shocking enough—but we are sincerely glad to hear all the good of them you send us. There is no chance I suppose, no <u>danger</u> of poor Mrs H.s being persuaded to come to Chawton at present.—I hope John H. will not have more debts brought in, than he likes.—I am pleased with M. T.'s being to dine at Steventon;—it may enable you to be yet more decided with Fanny & help to settle her faith.—Thomas was married on saturday, the wedding was kept at Neatham; & that is all I know about it.—Browning is quite a new Broom & at present has no fault. He had lost some of his knowledge of waiting, & is I think rather slow; but he is not noisy & not at all above being taught.—The Back gate is regularly locked.— I did not forget Henry's fee to Thomas.—I had a letter from Henry yesterday, written on sunday from Oxford; mine had been forwarded to him; Edward's information therefore ^was correct.—He says that Copies were sent to S. & P. at the same time with the others.—He has some thoughts of going to Adlestrop— [*end of p. 2; the rest of the letter is missing*]

Chawton Tuesday

This will be a quick return for your — I doubt its having much else to recommend saying, it may turn out to be a very long, a what a day was yesterday! How many imprints must have been confined — We felt of think of nothing to amuse you but packing. My Mother was quite in distress about Edw — ot be quite comfortable till she knows how ttled. — In a few hours you will be transp & then for London & Comfort & Coffee & C ill be your last visit there. — While I th ove to Alethea. (Alethea first, mind, sh eathcote & kind remembrance to Miss nly think of your having at last the d hat wonder of wonders her elder sister ou what you tell us of Deane. If Mrs Hea comfort him now, I shall think she is heart. — Really, either she or Alethea m where he is to look for Happiness? leard that you can say what you do, afte he whole work — & Fanny's praise is very pes were tolerably strong of her, but n & liking Darcy & Elizth is enough

Letter 7

INTRODUCTION

The final letter in this group, written 9 February 1813, is marked '4' on the address panel on p. 4. Cassandra Austen had by now moved from Steventon to Manydown, home of their old friends Alethea Bigg and her widowed sister Elizabeth (Mrs Heathcote). JA was still worrying over family responses to *Pride and Prejudice* and eager for praise, especially for the novel's central characters, Elizabeth Bennet and Mr Darcy.

your last visit there: old Mr Bigg-Wither was dying (d. 24 February 1813) and his daughters would expect to vacate the family home on that event. Elizabeth (Mrs Heathcote) and Alethea Bigg moved to Winchester whence they continued their friendship with JA and Cassandra.

what you tell us of Deane: Deane House, the Harwood estate very close to Steventon, where Cassandra has been staying. For the Harwoods, see the note to Letter 6.

Fanny's praise: Fanny Knight, JA's eldest niece and daughter of Edward (Austen) Knight.

the Boys: Edward Knight's sons, now pupils at Winchester College.

Sackree: Susannah Sackree, nursemaid since 1793 at Godmersham, Kent, Edward Knight's estate, and very much one of the family.

I shall tell Anna: her niece Anna Austen, who is to be let into the secret of her aunt's authorship.

My Uncle … in Pulteney S^t: the uncle and aunt referred to here are Mr and Mrs Leigh Perrot, JA's mother's brother and his wife, long-term residents in Bath. They owned Scarlets, in Berkshire, and after years of renting 1 Paragon in Bath had, in 1810–11, bought 49 Pulteney Street.

Charles: JA's youngest brother, now Captain Austen, with three daughters. His ship, HMS *Namur*, was based at the Nore, in the Thames Estuary.

Lady W.: presumably the wife of Charles's commander, Admiral Sir Thomas Williams.

Oath … Candle: an ancient Roman Catholic ritual of excommunication.

Quarto Volumes: JA teases her friends the Bigg sisters (with whom she can be sure Cassandra will share this letter) over the serious nature of their reading, and uses the opportunity to share another joke about the rival book societies of Alton and Steventon. Quarto format tended to be reserved for weighty, scholarly tomes (see the poem 'The Library' (1781) by JA's contemporary, George Crabbe, where 'quartos their well-order'd ranks maintain | And light octavos fill a spacious plain'). She takes the opportunity, too, to plug again her current favourite reading, Pasley's *Essay on … Military Policy* (see note to Letter 4).

Miss Edgeworth: a prolific Anglo-Irish novelist, JA's contemporary, and much admired by her. Edgeworth's latest work was *The Absentee*, in *Tales of Fashionable Life* (second series, 1812).

Mrs Grant: see note to Letter 4.

This will be a quick return for yours, my dear Cassandra; I doubt its' having much else to recommend it, but there is no saying, it may turn out to be a very long, delightful Letter. What a day was yesterday! How many impatient, grumbling spirits must have been confined!—We felt for you.—I could think of nothing to amuse you but packing up your cloathes. My Mother was quite in distress about Edward & Anna, & will not be quite comfortable till she knows how their Journeys were settled.—In a few hours you will be transported to Manydown—& then for Candour & Comfort & Coffee & Cribbage.—Perhaps it will be your last visit there.—While I think of it, give my Love to Alethea (Alethea first, mind, she is Mistress) & Mrs Heathcote—& kind remembrance to Miss Charlotte Williams. Only think of your having at last the honour of seeing that wonder of wonders her elder Sister!—We are very sorry for what you tell us of Deane. If Mrs Heathcote does not marry & comfort him now, I shall think she is a Maria & has no heart.—Really, either she or Alethea <u>must</u> marry him, or where he is [*sic*] to look for Happiness?—I am exceedingly pleased that you can say what you do, after having gone thro' the whole work—& Fanny's praise is very gratifying;—my hopes were tolerably strong of <u>her</u>, but nothing like a certainty. Her liking Darcy & Eliz^th is enough. She might hate all the others, if she would. [*p. 2*] I have her opinion under her own hand this morning, but your

Transcript of it which I read first, was not & is not the less acceptable.—To <u>me</u>, it is of course all praise—but the more exact truth which she sends <u>you</u> is good enough.—We are to see the Boys for a few hours this day se'night—& I am to order a Chaise for them—which I propose 5 o'clock for, & having a 3 o'clock dinner.—I am sorry to find that Sackree was worse again when Fanny wrote; she had been seized the night before with a violent shivering & Fever, & was still so ill as to alarm Fanny, who was writing from her room.—Miss Clewes seems the very Governess they have been looking for these ten years;—longer coming than J. Bond's last Shock of Corn.—If she will but only keep Good & Amiable & Perfect!—Clewes & [sic] is better than Clowes.—And is not it a name for Edward to pun on?—is not a Clew a Nail?—Yes, I beleive I <u>shall</u> tell Anna—& if you see her, & donot dislike the commission, you may tell her for me. You know that I meant to do it as handsomely as I could. But she will probably not return in time.—Browning goes on extremely well; as far as he has been able to do anything out of doors, my Mother is exceedingly pleased.—The Dogs seem just as happy with him as with Thomas;—Cook & Betsey I imagine a great deal happier.—Poor Cook is likely to be tried by a wet Season now; ^but she has not begun lamenting much yet.—Old Philmore I beleive is well again. [p. 3] My Cold has been an Off & on Cold almost ever since you went away, but never very bad; I increase it by walking out & cure it by staying within. On saturday I went to Alton, & the high wind made it worse—but by keeping house ever since, it is almost gone.—I have had Letters from my Aunt & from Charles within these few days.—My Uncle is quite confined to his Chair, by a broken Chilblain on one foot & a violent swelling in the other, which my Aunt does not know what to call;—there does not seem pain enough for Gout.—But you had all this history at Steventon perhaps.—She talks of being another fortnight at Scarlets; she is really anxious I can beleive to get to Bath, as they have an apprehension of their House in Pulteney S^t having been broken into.—Charles, his wife, & Eldest & Youngest reached the Namur in health & safety last Sunday se'night; Middle is left in Keppel S^t—Lady W. has taken to her old tricks of ill health again & is sent for a couple of Months among her friends. Perhaps she may make <u>them</u> sick.—I have been applied to for information as to the Oath taken in former times of Bell Book & Candle—but have none to give. Perhaps you may be able to learn something of its Origin & Meaning at Manydown.—Ladies who read those enormous, great stupid thick Quarto Volumes, which one always sees in the Breakfast parlour there, must be acquainted with every thing in the World.—I detest a Quarto.—Capt. Pasley's Book is too good for their Society. They will not understand a Man who condenses his Thoughts into an Octavo. [*p. 4*] I do not mean however to put Mrs H. out of conceit with her Society; if she is satisfied—well;—if she thinks others satisfied—still better;—I say nothing of the complaints which reach me from all quarters.—Kill poor Mrs Sclater if you like it, while you are at Manydown.—Miss Benn dined here on friday, I have not seen her since;—there is still work for one evening more.—I know nothing of the Prowtings. The Clements are at home & are reduced to read. They have got Miss Edgeworth.—I have disposed of Mrs Grant for the 2^d fortnight to Mrs Digweed;—it can make no difference to <u>her,</u> which of the 26 fortnights in the Year, the 3 vol^s lay in her House.—It is raining furiously—& tho' only a storm, I shall probably send my Letter to Alton instead of going myself.— I had no thought of your writing by Mr Gray; On Sunday or Tuesday I suppose I shall hear.—

Cook does not think the Mead in a state to be stopped down.

[continued upside down at the top of p. 1]
I do not know what Alethea's notions of Letter writing & Note writing may be, but <u>I</u> consider her as still in my Debt.—

[continued below address panel on p. 4]
 If Mrs Freeman is anywhere above Ground give my best Comp^{ts} to her.

Y^{rs} very affec^{ly}

J. Austen

[address panel reads]
Miss Austen
Manydown
By favour of
Mr Gray.

Sloane St. — Thursday

My dear Cassandra

Before I say anything else, I o
Halfpence on the Drawingroom Mantlepeie
myself & forgot to bring them with me. — I
ave yet been in any distress for Money, a
y due as well as the Devil. — How lucky,
eather yesterday! — This wet morning ma
ible of it. We had no rain of any conseq
te Curricle was put half-up three or four
hare of the Showers was very trifling, th
be heavy all round us, when we w
ack; & I fancied it might then be
t Chawton as to make you feel for us
e desired. — Three hours & a q[r]. took us
e staid barely two hours, & had only ju
'e we had to do there, that is, eating a
reakfast, watching the Carriages, paying
king a little stroll afterwards. From
t stroll gave us, I think most highly
Guildford —. We wanted all our Broth
nding with us in the Bowling Green
orsham. — I told Mr. Herington of the Cu
rually surprised & shocked, & means to b

Letter 8

INTRODUCTION

A letter from JA, who was staying with her brother Henry in Sloane Street, London, to Cassandra Austen, at home in Chawton, written 20 May 1813. She describes in some detail her journey with Henry from Chawton to London and her plans for shopping and a visit to an exhibition.

The letter descended through Charles Austen's branch of the family and was sold by his granddaughters in the 1920s. It was bought, after the Sotheby sale in 1948, by T. Edward Carpenter, and bequeathed by him to Jane Austen's House Museum in 1969. The address panel has the added inscription, in a later hand: 'From Sloane St | May 1813'. The letter has been sealed with a black wafer and has an indistinct postmark, including: 'Two Py Post Unpaid Sloane St'.

Curricle: a light, two-wheeled vehicle, with enough space for a driver and passenger.

Hog's-back: a narrow ridge of bare chalk hills, part of the Surrey North Downs and stretching between Farnham in the west and Guildford in the east, with extensive views over several counties.

M^r & Mrs Tilson: James Tilson was Henry Austen's partner in the Austen, Maunde & Tilson bank; they were neighbours, too, in Chelsea, London.

little Cass … two Betsies: 'little Cass' is Charles Austen's eldest child, Cassandra, staying with her nursemaid, Betsy, at Chawton Cottage, where there was another maid called Betsy. 'Cassy' is Edward Knight's daughter (another Cassandra), staying with her family at Chawton Great House.

Mrs Perigord … her Mother: also known as Mme Perigord, daughter of Mme Bigeon, a French émigrés and Henry Austen's housekeeper. JA was fond of Mme Bigeon, leaving her £50 in her will, the same amount as she left Henry. Henry's wife, Eliza, had died on 25 April 1813, and the household were in mourning (hence the black wafer used to seal the letter) but also busy preparing to move to 10 Henrietta Street, Covent Garden, which would be Henry's home as well as his office for the next months.

Water-coloured Exhibition: at 5 Spring Gardens, held
by the Society of Painters in Oil and Water Colours.

B^k Sarsenet: a fine fabric, often of silk.

Martha … £20,000: unless a joke, it sounds as though
Martha Lloyd, the other resident at Chawton Cottage, may
have won some money in the national lottery. There was an
English state lottery between 1694 and 1826.[1]

Mrs Craven … Charlotte: JA will later record in her 'Opinions of
Emma' (1816) that 'Mrs & Miss Craven - liked it very much,
but not so much as the others'.

NOTE

1   See Robin Vick, 'Some Unexplained References in JA's Letters',
    Notes & Queries, ns 41:3 (Sept. 1994), 318–21.

My dear Cassandra

Before I say anything else, I claim a paper full of Halfpence on the Drawingroom Mantlepeice; I put them there myself & forgot to bring them with me.—I cannot say that I have yet been in any distress for Money, but I chuse to have my due as well as the Devil.—How lucky we were in our weather yesterday!—This wet morning makes one more sensible of it. We had no rain of any consequence; the head of the Curricle was put half-up three or four times, but our share of the Showers was very trifling, though they seemed to be heavy all round us, when we were on the Hog'sback; & I fancied it might then be raining so hard at Chawton as to make you feel for us much more than we deserved.—Three hours & a q^r took us to Guildford, where we staid barely two hours, & had only just time enough for all we had to do there, that is, eating a long comfortable Breakfast, watching the Carriages, paying Mr Herington & taking a little stroll afterwards. From some veiws which that stroll gave us, I think most highly of the situation of Guildford. We wanted all our Brothers & Sisters to be standing with us in the Bowling Green & looking towards Horsham.—I told Mr Herington of the Currants; he seemed equally surprised & shocked, & means to talk to the Man who put them up. I wish you may find the Currants any better for it.—[*p. 2*] He does not expect Sugars to fall.—I was very lucky in my gloves, got them at the first shop I went to, though I went into it rather because it was near than because it looked at all like a glove shop, & gave only four Shillings for them;— upon hearing which, every body at Chawton will be hoping & predicting that they cannot be good for anything, & their worth certainly remains to be proved, but I think they look very well.—We left Guildford at 20 minutes before 12— (I hope somebody cares for these minutiae) & were at Esher in about 2 hours more.—I was very much pleased with the Country in general;—between Guildford & Ripley I thought it particularly pretty, also about Painshill & every where else; & from a Mr Spicer's Grounds at Esher which we walked into before our dinner, the veiws were beautiful. I cannot say what we did <u>not</u> see, but I should think there could not be a Wood or a Meadow or a Palace or a remarkable spot in England that was not spread out before us, on one side or the other.— Claremont is going to be sold, a Mr Ellis has it now;—it is a House that seems never to have prospered.—At 3, we were dining upon veal cutlets & cold ham, all very good; & after dinner we walked forward, to be overtaken at the Coachman's time, & before he <u>did</u> overtake us we were very near Kingston.—I fancy it was about ½ past 6 when we reached this house, a 12 hours Business, & the Horses did not appear more than reasonably tired. I was very tired too, & very glad to get to bed early, but am quite well to-day. [*p. 3*] Upon the whole it was an excellent Journey & very thoroughly enjoyed by me;— the weather was delightful the greatest part of the day, Henry found it too warm & talked of its' being close sometimes, but to my capacity it was perfection.—I never saw the Country from the Hogsback so advantageously.—We ate 3 of the Buns in the course of that stage, the remaining 3 made an elegant entertainment for M^r & Mrs Tilson who drank tea with us.— Now, little Cass & her attendant are travelling down to Chawton;—I wish the day were brighter for them. If Cassy should have intended to take any sketches while the others dine, she will hardly be able.—How will you distinguish the two Betsies?—Mrs Perigord arrived at ½ past 3—& is pretty well; & her Mother, for <u>her</u>, seems quite well. She sat with me while I breakfasted this morn^g—talking of Henrietta Street, servants & Linen; & is too busy in preparing for the future, to be out of spirits.—If I can, I shall call by & bye on Mrs Hoblyn & Charlotte Craven; Mrs Tilson is going out, which prevents my calling on <u>her</u>, but I beleive we are to drink tea with her.— Henry talks of our going to the Water-coloured Exhibition tomorrow, & of my calling for him in Henrietta S^t; if I do, I shall take the opportunity of getting my Mother's gown—; so, by 3 o'clock in the afternoon she may consider herself the owner of 7 y^{ds} of B^k Sarsenet as completely as I hope Martha finds herself of a 16th of the £20,000.—

    I am very snug with the front Drawingroom all to myself & would not say 'Thank you' for any companion but You. The quietness of it does me good.—Henry & I are disposed to wonder that the Guildford road should not be oftener preferred to the Bagshot, [*p. 4*] it is not longer, has much more beauty & not more hills.—If I were Charles, I should chuse it; & having him in our thoughts we made enquiries at Esher as to their posting distances.—From Guildford to Esher 14 miles, from Esher to Hyde Park corner 15—which makes it exactly the same as from Bagshot to H. P. corner, changing at Bedfont; 49 miles altogether, each way.—

I have contrived to pay my two visits, though the weather made me a great while about it, & left me only a few minutes to sit with C. C.—She looks very well & her hair is done up with an elegance to do credit to any Education. Her manners are as unaffected & pleasing as ever.—She had heard from her Mother today.—Mrs Craven spends another fortnight at Chilton.—I saw nobody but Charlotte, which pleased me best.—I was shewn up stairs into a Draw^g room, where she came to me, & the appearance of the room, so totally un-school-like amused me very much. It was full of all

[*continued below the address panel*]

the modern Elegancies—& if it had not been for some naked Cupids over the Mantlepeice, which must be a fine study for Girls, one should never have Smelt Instruction.

Mrs Perigord desires her Duty to all the Ladies.— Y^{rs} very affec^{ly} J. A.—

[*address panel reads*]
Miss Austen
Chawton
Alton
Hants

My dear Cassandra.

You were wrong in thinking o
night, we were at Cobham. On reaching G
the Horses were gone on. We therefore did
we had done at Farnham, sit in the Carr
were put in, & proceeded directly to Cobham, &
about 8 were sitting down to a very nice
had altogether a very good journey, & everythi
comfortable. — I could not pay Mr Herringto
only alas! of the Business. I shall therefore
my Mother's £2. — that you may try your x
begin reading till Bentley Green. Henry's a
even equal to my wishes; he says it is
the other two, but does not appear to think it
has only married Mrs R. I am afraid he has
most entertaining part. He took to Lady B
kindly, & gives great praise to the drawing
He understands them all, likes Fanny & a
it will all be. — I finished the Heroine
very much amused by it. I wonder Ja
better. It diverted me exceedingly. — W
o. I was very tired, but slept to a one
day; — & at present Henry seems to have
we left Cobham at ½ past 8, stopt to bai

Letter 9

A letter to Cassandra Austen in Chawton, written 2–3 March 1814, from Henry Austen's London address, 10 Henrietta Street, Covent Garden, where JA was overseeing the publication of *Mansfield Park*. It was her common practice to travel up to London with her manuscript and stay there during typesetting and proofing. She was in London between March and May 1811 with *Sense and Sensibility*. On this occasion she appears to have stayed there from 1 March until sometime in April; *Mansfield Park* was published 9 May 1814. To the modern reader this may seem an unusually compressed timeframe in which to turn manuscript into print, but in the 1810s it was not uncommon. It would not have been difficult to get 1,250 copies (the estimated run of the first edition of *Mansfield Park*) of a three-volume novel printed and ready for publication in two months, especially, as was the case here, with work divided between two printers. In the intervals between correcting proofs (the printed sheets would arrive in small batches every few days or even daily), there was time for shopping and visits to the theatre.

It is clear from JA's comments in this letter that her brother Henry, though acting as her agent in financial dealings over her novels, is even at this late stage, with the manuscript finished, reading *Mansfield Park* and discovering details of its characters and storyline for the first time. We know from other letters (see Letters 4 and 5) that Cassandra was privy to its development a year earlier. JA's comments on Henry's responses to the new novel cast a fascinating light on her own complex investment in this serious and moralizing novel, very different in tone from *Pride and Prejudice*.

The letter descended through Charles Austen's branch of the family and was sold by his granddaughters in the 1920s. It was bought by T. Edward Carpenter in 1952 from Eric Millar for £84, and bequeathed by him to Jane Austen's House Museum in 1969. The address panel has the added inscription: '1 From Hen:ta St | March 1814'.

Married M^{rs} R … M^{rs} N: Mrs Rushworth (the former Maria Bertram), Lady Bertram, Mrs Norris; all characters in *Mansfield Park*. JA goes on to mention others: Fanny Price and Henry Crawford.

the Heroine: *The Heroine; or, Adventures of a Fair Romance Reader*, by Eaton Stannard Barrett (1813), 'a delightful burlesque' or spoof Gothic novel, as JA says later in this letter.

Peace was generally expected: the Coalition army, led by General Blucher, was about to enter Paris. The Treaty of Fontainebleau, ending this phase of the war against Napoleon, was signed on 11 April.

twopenny post: the local London post, costing twopence from 1801, with letters picked up and delivered several times each day. Marianne Dashwood used it in *Sense and Sensibility*, ch. 26, to send a letter to Willoughby.

M^{de} B.: Madame Bigeon, Henry Austen's housekeeper; her daughter, Mme Perigord, is mentioned later in this letter. For both, see the note to Letter 8.

pair of Leaders: a pair of horses put in front of Henry's own, to ease the strain of pulling the carriage (*OED*, 'leader', sense 6b).

Keen: the actor Edmund Kean, who had made his first appearance at Drury Lane Theatre on 26 January as Shylock in Shakespeare's *The Merchant of Venice*. He was already the talk of the town.

Fanny: JA's twenty-one-year-old niece Fanny Knight.

Willow: pieces of plaited willow sold for hat-making.

wicked people Dyers are … in scarlet sin: JA, like all the Austens, enjoyed word games and puns. See her punning on the name of Miss Clewes, the new governess at Godmersham, in her letter of 9 February 1813 (Letter 7) and her thanks to Cassandra for the gift of charades, 29 January 1813 (Letter 5).

The Radcliffe style: that of Ann Radcliffe, a hugely successful writer of Gothic fiction (*The Romance of the Forest*, 1791, *The Mysteries of Udolpho*, 1794, *The Italian*, 1797). Catherine Morland of *Northanger Abbey* is a dedicated Radcliffe reader.

D'Syntax … Gogmagoglicus: references inserted to amuse 'little Cassandra', Charles Austen's daughter. William Combe, *The Tour of Dr Syntax in Search of the Picturesque* (1812), a comic poem, hugely popular owing to its engravings of the be-chinned cleric by Thomas Rowlandson. Dr Syntax visits London in cantos 22–25. Gogmagoglicus was a legendary giant; according to another tradition, he was two giants—Gog and his brother Magog—captured and made to serve as porters at the Guildhall, London, where their statues were still to be seen.

Henrietta St Wednesday March 2^d

My dear Cassandra

You were wrong in thinking of us at Guildford last night, we were at Cobham. On reaching G. we found that John & the Horses were gone on. We therefore did no more there than we had done at Farnham, sit in the Carriage while fresh Horses were put in, & proceeded directly to Cobham, which we reached by 7, & about 8 were sitting down to a very nice roast fowl &c.—We had altogether a very good Journey, & everything at Cobham was comfortable.—I could not pay Mr Herington!—That was the only alas! of the Business. I shall therefore return his Bill & my Mother's £2.—that you may try your Luck.—We did not begin reading till Bentley Green. Henry's approbation hitherto is even equal to my wishes;—he says it is very different from the other two, but ^does not appear to think it at all inferior. He has only married Mrs R. I am afraid he has gone through the most entertaining part.—He took to Lady B. & Mrs N. most kindly, & gives great praise to the drawing of the Characters. He understands them all, likes Fanny & I think foresees how it will all be.—I finished the Heroine last night & was very much amused by it. I wonder James did not like it better. It diverted me exceedingly.—We went to bed at 10. I was very tired, but slept to a miracle & am lovely today;—& at present Henry seems to have no complaints. We left Cobham at ½ past 8, stopt to bait &

breakfast at Kingston & were in this House considerably before 2—quite in the stile of Mr Knight. [*p. 2*] Nice smiling Mr Barlowe met us at the door, & in reply to enquiries after News, said that Peace was generally expected.—I have taken possession of my Bedroom, unpacked my Bandbox, sent Miss P.s two Letters to the twopenny post, been visited by M^de B.—& am now writing by myself at the new Table in the front room. It is snowing.—We had some Snow storms yesterday, & a smart frost at night, which gave us a hard road from Cobham to Kingston; but as it was then getting dirty & heavy, Henry had a pair of Leaders put on from the latter place to the bottom of Sloane S^t.—His own Horses therefore cannot have had hard work.—I watched for <u>Veils</u> as we drove through the Streets, & had the pleasure of seeing several upon vulgar heads.—And now, how do you all do? You in particular after the worry of yesterday & the day before. I hope Martha had a pleasant visit again, & that You & my Mother could eat your Beef pudding. Depend upon my thinking of the Chimney Sweeper as soon as I wake tomorrow.—Places are secured at Drury Lane for saturday, but so great is the rage for seeing Keen that only a 3^d & 4th row could be got. As it is in a front box however, I hope we shall do pretty well.—Shylock.—A good play for Fanny. She cannot be much affected I think.— Mrs Perigord has just been here. I have paid her a Shilling for the Willow. She tells me that we owe her Master for the Silk-dyeing.—My poor old Muslin has never been dyed yet; it has been promised to be done several times.—What wicked

People Dyers are. They begin with dipping their own Souls in Scarlet Sin.—Tell my Mother that my £6-15 was duly received, but placed to <u>my</u> account instead of hers, & I have just signed a something which makes it over to her. [*p. 3*] It is Even^g. We have drank tea & I have torn through the 3^d vol. of the Heroine, & do not think it falls off.—It is a delightful burlesque, particularly on the Radcliffe style.—Henry is going on with Mansfield Park; he admires H. Crawford—I mean properly— as a clever, pleasant Man.—I tell you all the Good I can, as I know how much you will enjoy it.—

John Warren & his wife are invited to dine here, to name their own day in the next fortnight.—I do not expect them to come.—Wyndham Knatchbull is to be asked for Sunday, & if he is cruel enough to consent, somebody must be contrived to meet him.—We hear that Mr Keen is more admired than ever. The two vacant places of our two rows, are likely to be filled by Mr Tilson & his Brother Genl Chownes.—I shall be ready to laugh at the sight of Frederick again.—It seems settled that I have the carriage on friday to pay visits, I have therefore little doubt of being able to get to Miss Hares. I am to call upon Miss Spencer: Funny me!—

There are no good Places to be got in Drury Lane for the next fortnight, but Henry means to secure some for Saturday fortnight when You are reckoned upon.—

I wonder what worse thing than Sarah Mitchell You are forced upon by this time!—Give my Love to little Cassandra, I hope she found my Bed comfortable last night & has not filled it with fleas.—I have seen nobody in London yet with such a long chin as D[r] Syntax, nor [*p. 4*] Anybody quite so large as Gogmagoglicus.—Yours affec[ly]

J. Austen

Thursday

My Trunk did not come last night, I suppose it will this morn[g]; if not—I must borrow Stockings & buy Shoes & Gloves for my visit. I was foolish not to provide better against such a Possibility. I have great hope however that writing about it in this way, will bring the Trunk presently.—

[*address panel reads*]
Miss Austen
Chawton
P[r] favor of
E. W. Gray Esq[re].

Dear Sir

My Emma is now so ne[ar]
that I feel it right to assure you [of my]
having forgotten your kind recom[mendation]
of an early copy for C. H. — [and of]
Mr. Murray's promise of its be[ing]
&[c]&[c] under cover to you, the[an at]
[the] Work being really out —

I must make use of this opportunity [to thank]
[you] dear Sir, for the very high praise you best[ow on my other]
Novels — I am too vain to wish to con[vince you that]
[you] have praised them beyond their Merit[s.]

My greatest anxiety at present is th[at this]
[4th] w[ork] not disgrace what was good in t[he others.]
[But on] this point I will do myself the just[ice to declare]
[th]at whatever may be my wishes [for its success,]
I am very strongly haunted by the [idea that to those]
[R]eaders who have preferred P & [P it will appear]
inferior in Wit, & to those who ha[ve preferred M P ve]-
[r]y inferior in good Sense. Such [differences as these]
however, I hope you will do me [the favor of ac]-
cepting a Copy. Mr M. will have [the pleasure]
[of] sending one. I am quite hon[oured by your]
thinking me capable of drawing such[...]

Letter 10

The next three letters form a group. *Emma*, JA's fourth novel
and last to appear in her lifetime, was published in late
December 1815, with a standard 1816 date on its title page.
JA was working with a new London publisher, John Murray.
Her brother Henry, her unofficial agent, was ill and more of
the negotiations than was usual fell to her; both she and
Murray were looking to make a social and critical splash with
this new novel and were actively concerned to market it well.
JA learned that the Prince Regent had read and admired her
novels and would be pleased to offer his patronage. This
unsought honour seems to have been a consequence of
Henry's illness: his physician, Dr Matthew Baillie, attended
members of the royal family and may have informed the
Regent of JA's presence in London. An invitation to visit
Carlton House, the Regent's London home, followed, issued
by his librarian, James Stanier Clarke, and permission to
'dedicate any future Work to HRH the P. R. without the
necessity of any Solicitation on my part' (JA to Clarke, 15
November 1815).

   It is unlikely that JA had changed her opinion of the
Regent since 16 February 1813 when she wrote to Martha

Lloyd of his very public rupture with his wife, Caroline of Brunswick: 'Poor woman, I shall support her as long as I can, because she <u>is</u> a Woman, & because I hate her Husband.' With the dedication, it is difficult to avoid the conclusion that she sacrificed scruples, artistic and political, in the hope that regal lustre might afford her commercial advantage. What rescues the situation is humour: the vacuous and repetitive terms of the dedication itself ('To | His Royal Highness| The Prince Regent, | This Work Is, | By His Royal Highness's Permission, | Most Respectfully | Dedicated, | By His Royal Highness's | Dutiful| And Obedient | Humble Servant, | The Author'), and the facetiousness of JA's correspondence with James Stanier Clarke. One result of which was the spoof 'Plan of a Novel, according to hints from various quarters', probably drafted in April 1816 as a comic release and private response to Clarke's daft suggestions.

All three letters descended through Charles Austen's branch of the family and were sold by his granddaughters in the 1920s. They were bought after the Sotheby's sale of 3 May 1948 by T. Edward Carpenter and bequeathed by him to Jane Austen's House Museum in 1969. The first in the series, written from Henry's home, 23 Hans Place, London, 11 December 1815, is JA's draft copy, never posted.

your note of Nov: 16: in which Clarke recommended that
JA describe 'in some future Work the Habits of Life and
Character and enthusiasm of a Clergyman—who should pass
his time between the metropolis & the Country … Fond of, &
entirely engaged in Literature—no man's Enemy but his own.'
There is a strong suggestion here and elsewhere that he was
offering himself as a worthy subject for a novel by Jane Austen!

Dear Sir

My Emma is now so near publication that I feel it right to assure you of my not having forgotten your kind recommendation of an early Copy for C. H.—& that I have Mr Murray's promise of its being sent to HRH. under cover to you, three days previous to the Work being really out.—

I must make use of this opportunity to thank you dear Sir, for the very high praise you bestow on my other Novels— I am too vain to wish to convince you that you have praised them beyond their Merit.—

My greatest anxiety at present is that this 4th work sh^d not disgrace what was good in the others. But on this point I will do myself the justice to declare that whatever may be my wishes for its' success, I am very strongly haunted by the idea that to those Readers who have preferred P&P. it will appear inferior in Wit, & to those who have preferred MP. very inferior in good Sense. Such as it is however I hope you will do me the favour of accepting a Copy. Mr M. will have directions for sending one. I am quite honoured by your thinking me capable of drawing such a Clergyman [*p. 2*] as you gave the sketch of in your note of Nov: 16. But I assure you I am <u>not</u>. The comic part of the Character I might be equal to, but not the Good, the Enthusiastic, the Literary. Such a Man's Conversation must at times be on subjects of Science &

Philosophy of which I know nothing—or at least be occasionally abundant in quotations & allusions, which a Woman, who like me, knows only her own Mother-tongue & has read very little in that, would be totally without the power of giving.—A Classical Education, or at any rate, a very extensive acquaintance with English Literature, Ancient & Modern, appears to me quite Indispensable for the person who w^d do any justice to your Clergyman—And I think I may boast myself to be, with all possible Vanity, the most unlearned, & uninformed Female who ever dared to be an Authoress.

Beleive me, dear Sir,
Your oblig^d & faith^l Hum. Servt.
J. A.

Pavilion –

Dear Miss Austen.   18

I have to return you
of His Royal Highness the
Regent for the handsom[e]
you sent him of your la[st]
Novel – pray dear M[iss]
soon write again and
Lord St Hellens and m[any]
the Nobility who have
staying here, said you
just tribute of their
The Prince Regent

Letter 11

The second letter in the series is not a direct reply (for that, see a letter of 21(?) December 1815, in *Jane Austen's Letters*, ed. Le Faye, p. 320) but sent some months later, from Brighton, acknowledging receipt of the copy of *Emma* sent to the Regent. Clarke persists in sending JA ideas for further novels.

An outer wrapper to the letter is held in the Morgan Library & Museum, New York. The letter was addressed to 'Miss Jane Austen | at Mr Murrays | Albemarle Street | London', from where it was readdressed to Henrietta Street, Henry Austen's business address, and subsequently to Chawton (see *Jane Austen's Letters*, ed. Le Faye, p. 456).

Pavilion: the letter was sent from Brighton Pavilion, the Regent's residence.

the Marriage: of the Regent's daughter, Princess Charlotte, and Prince Leopold of Saxe-Coburg, in May 1816.

Dear Miss Austen,

I have to return you the Thanks of His Royal Highness the Prince Regent for the handsome Copy you sent him of your last excellent Novel—pray dear Madam soon write again and again. Lord St Helens and many of the Nobility who have been staying here, paid you the just tribute of their Praise.

The Prince Regent has just [*p. 2*] left us for London; and having been pleased to appoint me Chaplain and Private English Secretary to the Prince of Cobourg, I remain here with His Serene Highness & a select Party until the Marriage. Perhaps when you again appear in print you may chuse to dedicate your Volumes to Prince Leopold: any Historical Romance illustrative of the History of the august house [*p. 3*] of Cobourg, would just now be very interesting.

Believe me at all times
Dear Miss Austen
Your obliged friend
J. S. Clarke

My dear Sir,

I am honoured by the Prin[ce]
am very much obliged to yourself for [the]
while you mention the work. [I]
acknowledge a former Letter, forwarded to [this]
Place. I assure you I felt very grateful [for the]
[ho]nor of it, & hope my silence will [not]
[be construed] it was truely meant, to proceed only [from un]
[will]ingness to tax your Time with idle [letters]
Under every interesting circumstance which
[your] literary Labours have placed you in, or
[the] Regent bestowed, you have — my bes[t]
[re]cent appointments I hope are a step [to]
In my opinion, not more truely should [be]
too well spard, for immense myriad[s] [to]
the Gospel, less baptize Gospel. [there]
[I] Time & Feeling required, but it
[i]n a [ ] live by it. Time will be
[the] sacrifice of Time & Feeling they m[ust be]
immense.

You are very, very kind in y[our]
the sort of Composition which might [be]
at present, & I am fully sensible th[at]

Letter 12

The third in the series, written 1 April 1816, is JA's draft copy, never posted. The letter contains JA's much-quoted defence of her particular style of writing: 'such pictures of domestic Life in Country Villages as I deal in'.

My dear Sir

I am honoured by the Prince's thanks, & ~~am~~ very much
obliged to yourself for the kind manner in which you mention
the Work.—I have also to acknowledge a former Letter,
forwarded to me from Hans Place. I assure You I felt very
grateful for the friendly Tenor of it, & hope my silence will
have been considered as it was truely meant, to proceed only
from an unwillingness to tax your Time with idle Thanks.—
Under every interesting circumstance which your own Talents
& literary Labours have placed you in, or the favour of the
Regent bestowed, you have my best wishes. Your recent
appointments I hope are a step to something ^still^ better. In my
opinion, The service of a Court can hardly be too well paid,
for immense must be the sacrifice of Time & Feeling required
by it.[1]

You are very, very kind in your hints as to the sort of
Composition which might recommend me at present, & I am
fully sensible that an Historical [*p. 2*] Romance, ~~on the History
of~~ ^founded on^ the House of Saxe Cobourg might be much more
to the purpose of Profit or Popularity, than such pictures of
domestic Life in Country Villages as I deal in—but I could no
more write a Romance than an Epic Poem.—I could not sit
seriously down to write a serious Romance under any other
motive than to save my Life, & if it were indispensable for me
to keep it up & never relax into laughing at myself or other
people, I am sure I should be hung before I had finished the

first Chapter.—No—I must keep to my own style & go on ^in
my own way;—and though I may never succeed again in that,
I am convinced that I should totally fail in any other.—

I remain my dear Sir,
Your very much obliged & very sincere friend

J. Austen

Chawton ^near Alton April 1st—
1816—

reunited to her there? — I know

me when my mind will be less

but I do not like to think of it.

less as on Earth, God grant th

to reflect on her as inhabiting ~~th~~

my humble endeavours (when it

join her there.

looking at a few of the precious paper

property I have # found some mea

which she desires that one of her gold che

her God-daughter Louisa & a lock of

now. You can read as whenever my

Letter 13

INTRODUCTION

Dated 29 July 1817, this is the second of two letters written by
Cassandra Austen to Fanny Knight in the days immediately
after JA's death. Fanny was JA's eldest niece and frequent
correspondent, described by her as 'the delight of my Life'
(letter of 20 February 1817). JA showed early symptoms of her
final illness in spring 1816 and battled with slow degeneration
and occasional periods of recovery for the next year. She made
her will on 27 April 1817; on 24 May she and Cassandra left
Chawton to seek medical attention in Winchester, lodging at
8 College Street. Cassandra nursed her until the end, which
came in the early hours of 18 July. Cassandra had first written
to Fanny from Winchester on 20 July: 'I <u>have</u> lost a treasure,
such a Sister, such a friend as never can have been
surpassed,—She was the sun of my life, the gilder of every
pleasure, the soother of every sorrow, I had not a thought
concealed from her, & it is as if I had lost a part of myself.'
At home once more in Chawton, she wrote now of JA's funeral
and, movingly, of her own fortitude and Christian conviction
in the face of loss. As a female relative she was excluded, by
convention, from accompanying her sister's body to the grave;
hence her remark about watching 'the little mournful

procession the length of the Street' until it disappeared from sight and 'I had lost her forever'.

The letter was inherited by Fanny Knight's son, Lord Brabourne, who sold it at auction with others in 1893. In the 1930s it came into the possession of the Shakespeare scholar and Austen enthusiast, Professor Caroline Spurgeon, who bequeathed it to the medieval scholar Helen Waddell; thereafter it was in other private hands until purchased in 2015 by Jane Austen's House Museum with Heritage Lottery Fund support, a grant from Friends of the National Libraries and wider public support (for fuller provenance, see *Jane Austen's Letters*, ed. Le Faye, p. 468).

Chawton Tuesday

My dearest Fanny

I have just read your letter for the third time & thank you most sincerely for every kind expression to myself & still more warmly for your praises of her who I believe was better known to you than to any human being besides myself. Nothing of the sort could have been more gratifying to me than the manner in which you write of her & if the dear Angel is conscious of what passes here & is not above all earthly feelings, she ~~must~~ ˄ᵐᵃʸ ᵖᵉʳʰᵃᵖˢ receive pleasure in being so mourned. Had <u>she</u> been the survivor I can fancy her speaking of <u>you</u> in almost the same terms—there are certainly many points of strong resemblance in your characters—in your intimate acquaintance with each other & your mutual strong affection you were counterparts. [*p. 2*] Thursday was not so dreadful a day to me as you imagined, there was so much necessary to be done that there was not time for additional misery. Every thing was conducted with the greatest tranquility, & but that I was determined I would see the last & therefore was upon the listen, I should not have known when they left the House. I watched the little mournful procession the length of the Street & when it turned from my sight & I had lost her for ever—even then I was not overpowered, nor so much agitated as I am now in writing of it.—Never was human being more sincerely mourned by those who attended her remains than was this dear creature. May the sorrow with which she is parted from on earth be a prognostic of the joy with which she is hailed in Heaven!—I continue very tolerably well, much better than any one could have supposed possible, because I certainly have had considerable fatigue of body as well as anguish of [*p. 3*] mind for months back, but I really am well, & I hope I am properly grateful to the Almighty for having been so supported. Your Grandmama too is much better than when I came home.—I did not think your dear Papa appeared unwell, & I understand that he seemed much more comfortable after his return from Winchester than he had done before. I need not tell you that he was a great comfort to me—indeed I can never say enough of the kindness I have received from him & from every other friend.—I get out of doors a good deal & am able to employ myself. Of course those employments suit me best which leave me most at leisure to think of her I have lost & I do think of her in every variety of circumstance. In our happy hours of confidential intercourse, in the chearful family party, which she so ornamented, in her sick room, on her death bed & as (I hope) an inhabitant of Heaven. Oh! If I may one day [*p. 4*] be reunited to her there!—I know the time must come when my mind will be less engrossed by her $_\wedge$^{idea}, but I do not like to think of it. If I think of her less as on Earth, God grant that I may never cease to reflect on her as inhabiting ~~the~~ Heaven & never cease my humble endeavours (when it shall please God) to join her there.

In looking at a few of the precious papers which are now my property I have found some Memorandums, amongst which she desires that one of her gold chains may be given to her God-daughter Louisa & a lock of her hair be set for you. You can need no assurance my dearest Fanny that every request of your beloved Aunt will be sacred with me. Be so good as to say whether you prefer a broche or ring.

[*continued below the address panel*]
God bless you my dearest Fanny. Believe me most affect[^ly]
Yours

Cass. Eliz[^th] Austen.

[*address panel reads*]
Miss Knight
Godmersham Park
Canterbury.

FURTHER READING

Jane Austen's Letters, ed. Deirdre Le Faye, 4th edition, Oxford University Press, Oxford, 2011.

James Edward Austen-Leigh, *A Memoir of Jane Austen and Other Family Recollections*, ed. Kathryn Sutherland, Oxford University Press, Oxford, 2002.

Paula Byrne, *The Real Jane Austen: A Life in Small Things*, HarperPress, London, 2013.

Jan Fergus, *Jane Austen: A Literary Life*, Palgrave Macmillan, Basingstoke, 1991.

Deidre Lynch, 'The Art of the Letter', in Kathryn Sutherland (ed.), *Jane Austen: Writer in the World*, Bodleian Publications, Oxford, 2017.

Lindsay O' Neill, *The Opened Letter: Networking in the Early Modern British World,* University of Pennsylvania Press, Philadelphia, 2015.

Howard Robinson, *The British Post Office: A History*, Princeton University Press, Princeton, New Jersey, 1948.

Amanda Vickery, *The Gentleman's Daughter: Women's Lives in Georgian England*, Yale University Press, London and New Haven, CT, 1998.

INDEX

Jane Austen is JA throughout. FK denotes Fanny Knight.

Adlestrop, Gloucestershire 76, 79
Alton Book Society 55, 57, 83, 86
Alton, Hampshire 64, 78, 85
Austen, Anna (niece) 25, 60, 67, 82, 84, 85
Austen, Caroline (niece) 24–5, 69, 72
Austen, Cassandra
    Chawton Cottage, Hampshire 49
    and *Emma* 68
    letters from JA 18, 23–6, 55, 81, 89, 97
    letters to FK 121–2
Austen, Cassandra (d. of Charles) 90, 94,
    101, 105
Austen, Cassandra (mother) 51, 55, 61, 68,
    77, 84, 94
Austen, Charles
    and JA 94–5
    letters from JA 25, 39, 56, 86
    naval career 37, 42, 60, 65, 82
Austen, Edward (nephew) 25, 84
Austen, Eliza (wife of Henry) 90
Austen, Fanny (1st wife of Charles) 53
Austen, Francis William (nephew) 49, 52
Austen, Frank 25, 26, 36, 40, 49–53, 70
Austen, Henry
    and Charles 70
    gifts from 55, 61
    homes 24, 90, 99, 108
    JA's agent 15, 67–8, 97, 107
    journeys with JA 93–4, 102–3
Austen, James 55, 69, 70, 102
Austen, Mary (1st wife of Frank) 52, 55,
    64, 70
Austen, Revd George 26, 35, 40, 62

Baillie, Dr Matthew 107
Barrett, Eaton Stannard 99
Barrow, John 59
Bath 26, 35–6, 82
Benn, Miss 56, 62, 64–5, 70, 72, 77, 86
Betsey (maid) 16, 69, 85, 90
Bigeon, Mme 90, 99
Bigg, Althea 55, 81, 83, 84, 87

Bigg, Catherine 45–7
Bigg-Wither, Harris 45, 81
Bond, John 59, 70, 85
Brabourne, Edward, Lord 122
Bramston family 63, 65
Browning (manservant) 16, 76, 79, 85
Buchanan, Claudius 58

Caroline, of Brunswick 108
Carpenter, T. Edward 45, 50, 56, 67, 89,
    98, 108
Carr, Sir John 61, 62
Carter, Thomas (manservant) 16, 62, 79
Chamberlayne, Mrs 39
Chawton Cottage, Hampshire 16–18, 49
Chawton House, Hampshire 51
Chute, William John 57, 61
Claremont House, Surrey 93
Clarke, James Stanier 16, 25, 107–11, 114,
    118–19
Clarkson, Thomas 58
Clement family 62, 64
Clewes, Miss (governess) 85, 100
Cobham, Surrey 102
Combe, William 101
'Cook' 16, 85, 87
Cottrell, Mr 65
Coulthard family 63
Crabbe, George 83
Craven, Charlotte 94, 95
Craven, Martha 39, 95

Deane House, Hampshire 81, 84
Digweed family 56, 61, 63, 72, 87
Drury Lane Theatre, London 103, 104
Dummer, Hampshire 56, 75, 77

Edgeworth, Maria 83, 87
Egerton, Thomas 67
Emma
    characters in 19–21, 24, 29–30
    publication of 68, 107, 110, 113

Esher, Surrey 93, 95
Evelyn family 36–7, 40–1, 43

Fowle, Tom 35
Fust, Lady 39

Gauntlett, Mr 63
George, Prince Regent 107–8, 110, 113, 114
Godmersham, Kent 24, 70, 82
Grant, Anne 58, 87
Guildford, Surrey 92–3

Harwood family 76, 78–9
Heathcote, Elizabeth (née Bigg) 36, 40, 55,
    71, 76, 81, 83
Herington, Mr 92, 102
Hogan, Charles Beecher 37
Holder family 39–40

Jane Austen Society 26, 37, 51

Kean, Edmund 100, 103, 104
Kintbury, Berkshire 35, 39–43
Knatchbull, Wyndham 104
Knight, Cassandra 90, 94
Knight, Edward (Austen) 24, 49, 76, 79,
    82, 85
Knight, Fanny (niece) 25–6, 81, 84–5, 103,
    121–5

Le Faye, Deirdre 51, 59, 68
Leigh Perrot, James (uncle) 35, 82, 86
Leigh Perrot, Jane 35–6, 65, 82, 86
Leopold, Prince 114
Littleworth, Elizabeth 51
Littleworth, John 51
Lloyd, Martha
    away from home 39, 59, 64–5, 78
    friend of JA 36, 72
    lottery winner 91, 94
Lloyd, Mary 45
Lyncombe & Widcombe, Bath 39
Lysons, Mrs 40

Macartney, George 59
Mansfield Park
    characters in 37, 57–9, 69, 99, 102, 104
    publication of 68, 75, 97–8
    readers and 110
Manydown House, Hampshire 55, 78, 86

Mapleton, Christiana 40
Mapleton, Jane 40
Mapleton, Marianne 40
Mowll, Rosemary 50
Murray, John 25, 107, 110
Mussell, Mrs 43

Napoleonic Wars 38, 57, 99
Northanger Abbey 36, 100

Papillon family 56, 62, 63, 64
Pasley, Captain Charles 57, 61, 83, 86
Perigord, Mme Marie 90, 94, 95, 103
Philips, Mr 41
Piozzi, Hester Thrale 38
Portsmouth, Hampshire 70
Pride and Prejudice
    characters in 68, 76, 78, 81, 84
    publication of 55, 67–8, 75–8
    readers and 110

Radcliffe, Ann 100
Rowlandson, Thomas 101

Sackree, Susannah (nursemaid) 82, 85
Scarlets, Berkshire 65, 82, 86
Scott, Walter 50, 68
Sense and Sensibility 67, 97, 99
Shakespeare, William 57, 100
Sibley sisters 63–4
Smith, James and Horatio 58
Southey, Robert 45
Spurgeon Caroline 122
Steventon, Hampshire 26, 35, 70
Steventon Rectory, Hampshire 55, 69

Terry family 56, 65, 75
Terry, Michael 56, 65
Terry, Patience 56, 63
Tilson, Frances 94
Tilson, James 90, 94
Twyford, Mr 62

Waddell, Helen 122
Warren, John 104
Williams, Admiral Sir Thomas 82
Williams, Charlotte 84
Williams, Lady 82, 86
Wood, Miss 43